Sweets
on a
Stick

More Than
150 Kid-Friendly
Recipes for Cakes, Candies, Cookies, and Pies
on the Go!

Linda Vandermeer

adamsmedia

Avon, Massachusetts

Published by
Adams Media, a division of F+W Media, Inc.
57 Littlefield Street, Avon, MA 02322. U.S.A.
www.adamsmedia.com

ISBN 10: 1-4405-3005-X
ISBN 13: 978-1-4405-3005-0
eISBN 10: 1-4405-3135-8
eISBN 13: 978-1-4405-3135-4

Printed in the United States of America.

10   9   8   7   6   5   4   3   2   1

Library of Congress Cataloging-in-Publication Data
is available from the publisher.

This publication is designed to provide accurate and authoritative information with regard to the subject matter covered. It is sold with the understanding that the publisher is not engaged in rendering legal, accounting, or other professional advice. If legal advice or other expert assistance is required, the services of a competent professional person should be sought.
—From a *Declaration of Principles* jointly adopted by a Committee of the American Bar Association and a Committee of Publishers and Associations

Many of the designations used by manufacturers and sellers to distinguish their product are claimed as trademarks. Where those designations appear in this book and Adams Media was aware of a trademark claim, the designations have been printed with initial capital letters.

Photos by Linda Vandermeer and Terri Vandermeer

*This book is available at quantity discounts for bulk purchases.
For information, please call 1-800-289-0963.*

Dedication

For my family, Craig, Lilli, Sophie, and Robert, who inspire and support every sweet thing I do.

Acknowledgments

I would like to thank Andrea, my editor, who pulled this book together from start to finish under extremely tight deadlines, and the rest of the team at Adams Media for their contributions and support.

My thanks go to all of these people as well:

Terri Vandermeer, whose photography captured the fun and spirit of the treats I created.

My husband, Craig, who took the kids to the park every weekend so I could rewrite and test recipes.

My amazing mum and dad for making me who am I.

Sue S, for peeking into her pantry for me.

Lorainne @ Not Quite Nigella, for my first-ever blog comment, which kept me going at the start.

Naomi V, Elizabeth M, Missus T, and Caroline S who do what they love with a passion, which inspired me to do the same.

And my blog and Facebook followers, who constantly make me want to create that next, even more exciting treat to share.

Contents

CHAPTER 3: CUPCAKE POPS 52

CHAPTER 4: COOKIE POPS 63

CHAPTER 5: OUTSIDE-THE-BOX POPS 107

CHAPTER 6: CUTIE PIE POPS 127

CHAPTER 7: FRUIT ON A STICK 141

CHAPTER 8: CANDY ON A STICK 152

CHAPTER 9: THE ICING ON THE CAKE 162

CHAPTER 10: DECORATING AND DISPLAYING YOUR POPS ... 167

Introduction

Why are we so fascinated with food on sticks? What is it about popping food on a stick that makes it so much cuter?

Put a treat on a stick and all of a sudden it POPS! It's as if those sticks are magic wands whisking away the everyday and replacing it with fabulous and fun yumminess fit for a celebration.

There will be no more telling the kids not to play with their food with these super-delicious sweets on a stick. From creepy ghouls to fairy bites, not only will your kids love spending time in the kitchen baking these creations; they'll also love playing with the fabulous results.

Flying butterfly wands fluttering from flower to flower, crazy cake pop cars zooming around, or invading aliens visiting from Mars—the possibilities are there for endless imaginative play and creative development.

So many of the recipes in this book make the perfect activity for a play date or party. Invite kids of all ages to make, bake, and decorate—then sit back and watch as they laugh and play with the unique results. It's just plain fun for everyone involved, even though there might be a little extra cleaning up afterward with kids in the kitchen!

From tots to teens, there are techniques included to suit every age and skill level. Younger kids will delight in sifting, mixing, adding ingredients, and trying out some of the simple decorating ideas, while the more advanced crowd will be able to whip up whole projects.

Getting kids involved in the kitchen doesn't just teach them to cook, it helps their development in so many other ways. They have to follow directions while reading a recipe, count items to be included, and watch what happens when ingredients mix together. They learn how to do things in the correct order and find there are possible consequences if they don't. Older kids will learn about the chemistry involved in mixing the different ingredients and how they react to each other. There are countless opportunities to expand children's minds when working through the methods found in this book.

Also, when kids are part of the process of creating new foods they are more likely to try out the results— although with all of the delicious recipes in this book it won't be hard to find something that you will all love. From fruity to chocolate, crunchy to smooth, there are dozens of tasty bites to tempt your taste buds.

With these fun, easy, and fabulous recipes for treats on a stick in this book, you and your children will be chatting and interacting over the mixing bowl in no time. Together you will not just be making sweets on a stick to eat, you will also be making memories that will last a lifetime.

CHAPTER 1

Equipment and Ingredients

This book is about having fun baking with your family and not about buying stacks of stuff you might never use again or spending time online searching for special ingredients. Most of the recipes in this book do not call for equipment or ingredients that are hard to find. Where a recipe has specialty equipment listed, there is generally a tip on how to work around it using items that are easy to find in your home or in grocery or craft stores.

Lollipop Sticks

If you want to put your treats on a stick, you need good-quality lollipop sticks. Be sure to use lollipop sticks that are paper based and baking safe. You can find them in a variety of sizes, but unless the recipe calls for a specific size, plan on using 6" sticks for all of your pops. Lollipop sticks also come in a variety of thicknesses. In most instances, and unless the recipe specifies otherwise, the thickness does not matter. You can find lollipop sticks at specialty cake- and chocolate-making stores, craft stores, and many online stores including Amazon, eBay, and Etsy.

Cake Pop Stand

A number of manufacturers now make cake pop stands, which are reusable plastic or acrylic trays with premade holes that will hold your cake pops and other treats both while you decorate them and through the setting process. They are available from specialty cake stores, eBay, and online stores.

Cookie Cutters

Cookie cutters of all shapes and sizes are handy when it comes to making cookie pops. You can find them relatively low-priced at kitchen supply shops or even discount stores. Some wholesale companies even sell the same cutter shape in different sizes. Try checking out discount racks after the holidays to find shapes you wouldn't normally find during the year. Cutters come in metal or plastic, and both have their advantages. Metal cutters are sturdier and have sharper edges, while plastic cutters are generally less expensive and easier to keep clean. Some cutters come with a rubber handgrip or handle attached, which can make it easier for small children to use. Unless the cutter you buy states otherwise, do not put cookie cutters in the dishwasher. Many of the recipes in this book use a 3" round cutter, but if you don't have one you can use the top of a clean plastic cup in a pinch.

Wooden Skewers

Some of the recipes call for wooden skewers instead of lollipop sticks. Wooden skewers are easier to use for recipes like Rainbow Fruit Kabobs because paper lollipop sticks might get too soggy. Make sure your wooden skewers are foodsafe. If you buy them from a craft section of a store rather than the food section, they may be treated with harmful chemicals. No matter where you get them, it is always a good idea to cut the pointed ends off the skewers when young kids will be having the treats. Be sure to supervise your children at all times while they are handling the skewers.

Pastry Pedestals

While not necessary for most of the recipes in this book, this neat gadget allows you to pop nearly any sweet treat onto a stick. The Pastry Pedestal is a stick with a mini round plate at the top. You can adjust the round plate up and down to leave a small portion of the stick poking up to which you secure your treat. The treat then rests on the small round plate. It's great for holding treats that need a bit more support. Check out the suppliers and mail order sources section to find out where to buy a Pastry Pedestal.

Paper Baking Cups

Foodsafe paper baking cups come in large, medium, and small sizes and a wide range of colors, including special holiday patterns. Generally this book calls for the mini or small sizes. When picking patterned cups, remember that the cake batter will darken most light colors. You can purchase baking cups at local supermarkets, craft stores, and online.

Microwave

Most of the recipes in this book call for melting chocolate or heating ingredients in a microwave. If you don't have a microwave, you can still follow every recipe by heating ingredients on a stovetop using a saucepan or, in the case of chocolate, a double boiler.

Double Boiler

Although not essential if you have a microwave, a double boiler can be useful. A double boiler is a set of two saucepans that fit together. You fill the bottom saucepan with a small amount of water and set it to simmer. The ingredient that you need to melt goes into the second saucepan, which fits securely into the bottom pan, leaving enough space so that the simmering water does not touch the bottom the pan. Using this method ensures that the ingredients melt over gentle heat, which is preferred for chocolate work. If you do not have a double boiler, you can place a heat-safe bowl on top of a saucepan of simmering water. Ensure that the bowl is a snug fit and that none of the simmering water can escape into the chocolate as even a drop of water can cause the chocolate to seize up and make it unusable for dipping.

Electric Mixer

Many of the recipes use an electric mixer, which can be either a stand mixer or a hand-held mixer. Using a KitchenAid stand mixer with a pouring shield makes it easier for little helpers to add the ingredients. However, never leave the mixer unattended when it's plugged in, as the temptation to stick little fingers in the bowl is too great.

Fondant Cutters

Just like cookie cutters, fondant cutters come in many shapes and sizes and are used to cut decorating fondant into uniform shapes. Fondant cutters are usually smaller than cookie cutters. In addition to plain cutters, you can buy ejector fondant cutters, which emboss a pattern onto the fondant as well as cutting shapes like butterflies and snowflakes. You can find fondant cutters and ejectors at specialty cake stores, large craft and hobby stores, online stores, and on eBay.

Rolling Pin

If you don't already have one, buy a wooden or plastic rolling pin that is easy for children to handle for rolling out cookie dough. If you are doing fondant work on cookies, it's a good idea to use a smaller plastic rolling pin as it is easier to handle, less likely to stick, and will not leave any wood texture marks on the fondant. You can purchase rolling pins at specialty cake stores, large craft and hobby stores, online stores, and on eBay.

Sifter

A sifter is used in many of the recipes to break up any lumps in flour or sugar mixtures and to help distribute dry ingredients. If you do not have a sifter, a large metal mesh strainer can be used by pushing any ingredient through with the back of a large spoon.

Styrofoam Block

A 12" × 12" block of Styrofoam, 2" to 3" thick, is invaluable when you are dipping cake pops and other treats. After dipping, just poke the stick into the Styrofoam, and the treat will set properly without being disturbed. You can purchase Styrofoam blocks at large craft stores and online.

Bowls

A variety of bowls in different sizes will be helpful. If you have a stand mixer, it should already have a large, deep bowl, but if not, be sure you have one large enough for mixing batches of cake batter and cookie dough. If you plan to make cake pops, you'll also need microwave-safe bowls that are small enough for melting candy and chocolate but still deep enough for dipping. With little

hands helping it is safer to choose materials that are less likely to break, like sturdy microwave-safe plastic.

Cookie Sheets and Pans

The recipes in this book call for flat, sturdy cookie sheets for baking cookies, and a selection of baking pans including mini-cupcake or muffin pans, 8" round baking pans, 8" square pans, and a 9" round spring-form pan. Purchase nonstick bakeware if possible to make it easier to release baked goods from the pans and clean up afterward. The baking temps given in the recipes are for metal pans. If you are using glass bakeware, reduce the oven temperature by 25 degrees.

Parchment Paper

Disposable parchment paper is used for lining cookie sheets to reduce the chance of food items sticking. Wax paper is not a suitable replacement for parchment paper when the paper will be placed in the oven. Parchment paper is available from grocery stores.

Piping Bags and Tips

Piping bags (or pastry bags), which can be made of disposable plastic or a reusable material, are triangular-shaped bags with a hole at the narrow end that allows you to squeeze frosting or icing neatly and decoratively on treats. You can choose from a variety of metal or plastic tips for the piping bag to achieve the decorative finish you want. A number of the recipes in this book mention using piping bags and specific piping tips, but an alternative is always given in case you don't have this equipment. You can purchase piping bags and tips at specialty cake stores, large craft and hobby stores, online stores, and through eBay and Amazon.

Ingredients

Candy Coating

Also known as confectionery coating, candy melts, or candy wafers, this is a chocolate substitute with a low cocoa-butter content, making it more stable and easier to use than regular chocolate. Candy coating also sets faster and harder than regular chocolate, which makes it perfect for dipping pops. There is a wide variety of brands, in a range of colors and qualities. Some popular brands include Wilton Candy Melts, Make 'n' Mold, and Merckens Confectionery Coating. You can find candy coating at specialty cake- and chocolate-making stores, craft stores, and many online stores, including Amazon, eBay, and Etsy. See Melting Tips in Chapter 2 to assure best results.

Candy Writer

A candy writer is an easy-to-use disposable tube that is filled with candy coating. You just need to insert the tube into warm water to melt the candy coating, remove the covering tip, and snip off the end with scissors. By replacing the covering tip securely you can remelt or store the candy writers for later use.

Candy

The recipes in this book call for a wide variety of candies to use as flavoring and decorations. All of them are widely available and should be easily found in your supermarket. Candy brands and types used for decoration can be substituted with a similar type of candy with no impact on the recipes in this book.

Sprinkles, Sugar Confetti, and Nonpareils

Sprinkles are small edible sugary confectionery used for decorating food. They come in an almost endless range of shapes, flavors, and colors. Some popular shapes for sprinkles include hearts, stars, and flowers. Other types of sprinkles include jimmies and sanding sugar. Sugar confetti are multicolored edible sugar-based discs that look like little rounds of real confetti. Unless specified, do not substitute jumbo confetti sprinkles. Nonpareils are small round sugar sprinkles that come in a range of sizes. All are available from grocery stores, specialty cake- and chocolate-making stores, craft stores, and many online stores, including Amazon, eBay, and Etsy.

Edible Food Marker

Just like a regular marker but with edible ink, edible food markers can be purchased individually or in sets like ink markers. You can use them to draw on any hard, dry surface, including dried Marshmallow Fondant and Royal Icing. Food markers often contain the same additives as food color, so take care to read the labels if there are any allergy sufferers in your household. Wilton FoodWriter, Americolor Gourmet Writer, and FooDoodler are popular brands. You can purchase them at specialty cake stores, large craft and hobby stores, and online through Amazon and eBay.

Food Color

Food color comes in a wide range of mediums. Gel food colors are recommended in this book for all non-chocolate work as they give a bright, even color without adding too much extra liquid. Specialty oil-based colors are required when coloring chocolate, as water-based colors will cause chocolate to seize, making it unworkable. Wilton and Americolor are popular brands of gel food color. You can purchase both the gel- and oil-based colors at specialty cake stores, large craft and hobby stores, online, and through Amazon and eBay.

Luster Spray

This shimmery edible food color comes in an easy-to-use spray can, just like paint, making it simple to add accents to all types of food treats. PME is a popular brand. Luster spray is available from craft stores, online specialty cake shops, eBay, and Amazon.

Marshmallow Fondant

Marshmallow Fondant is a decorating medium made by melting marshmallow and mixing it with powdered sugar. When made correctly the fondant should be pliable, similar to Play-Doh, and can be rolled out with a rolling pin and cut to shape to make edible decorations. A recipe is included in Chapter 9. Store-bought ready-to-roll fondant brands like Wilton and Satin Ice, which can be purchased from specialty cake stores and craft stores, can be substituted in place of Marshmallow Fondant for any of the recipes in this book.

Meringue Powder

Meringue powder includes egg whites along with other ingredients and is commonly used to make royal icing. It is available from craft stores and online specialty cake shops.

Paramount Crystals

Paramount crystals are flavor-free chips of palm kernel oil with other additives that can be added to chocolate or candy coating during the melting process to help make the mixture smoother and more fluid. This results in a smoother finish to cake pops and other treats. This product helps the candy coating keep its fast-setting properties. If you are unable to find this product, you can substitute vegetable shortening. The amount of crystals or shortening you'll need will vary between candy coating brands. A safe estimate is 1 ounce to 2 ounces of crystals or shortening per 14-ounce bag of candy coating. Start with 1 ounce and add more during the melting process as required. You can purchase paramount crystals at specialty cake and chocolate stores, online, and through Amazon and eBay.

Premade Sugar Decorations

Premade sugar decorations come in a multitude of shapes and colors and make decorating easy. Usually made from colored royal icing and then dried, these decorations are edible and have a long shelf life. Popular shapes include butterflies, flowers, lady beetles, and eyes. You can use premade sugar decorations for any recipes in this book that suggest making your own marshmallow fondant decorations. Wilton is a well-known brand. You can find sugar decorations at specialty cake stores, craft and hobby stores, online, and from Etsy and eBay.

Safety in the Kitchen

Cooking is great fun, but as with everything, it's not without its dangers. Be sure to keep these tips in mind:

Never leave younger children in the kitchen with something on the stove or an electrical appliance switched on.

- Some of the recipes in this book require food to be heated in the microwave. ALWAYS check how hot any item is before letting the kids start to work with it.

- Follow manufacturers' instructions with all electrical appliances.

- Make sure children know to stand clear when you're taking hot items out of the microwave or oven, or off the stove.

- If children are not tall enough to reach the countertop, provide a stable, child-suitable step for them to use. If you can't do that, take the baking to them. You can even sift, mix, and add ingredients while sitting together on the floor in your kitchen, and you can decorate cookies on a smaller table they can easily reach.

- Follow safe food practices. Be sure to wash hands, work surfaces, and countertops often, and store perishable food in the refrigerator.

CHAPTER 2

Cake Pops

Are you ready to join the cake pop revolution? Cake pops consist of cake and frosting mixed together to form ball shapes that can be put on a stick and decorated. In this chapter you will learn how to make basic cake pops. You'll find a few no-fail recipes for the cake base, discover a bunch of great dipping tips, and get a stack of easy instructions on how to turn the plain pops into fun, creative pop masterpieces. So, let's start at the beginning—making the perfect cake for cake pops!

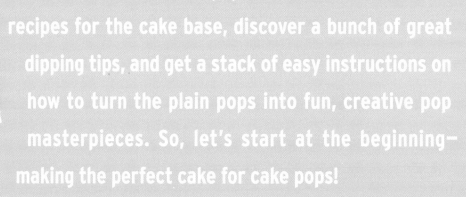

MAKING THE CAKE

Every great cake pop needs a base. You can use any flavor you want, but there are suggested flavors found in each of the decorating recipes. You'll also find recipes for dairy-free and gluten-free cake just in case you're making pops for people who have allergies. All the cake recipes in this chapter will make an 8" cake, enough for 20 to 30 cake balls. If you like, you can use a premade or box mix cake. Just follow the same process described here and adjust the frosting to make the mixture the right texture.

Quick and Easy Vanilla Cake

This recipe will yield 28 pops with the addition of ¾ cup of frosting and 18 ounces of candy coating for dipping.

This scrumptious vanilla cake is the perfect base for many of your cake pops and it can be made in one bowl, which means less time cleaning and more time eating! Make sure the butter is very soft, as there is no creaming step. If it's a cold day or you're pressed for time, you can cut the butter into cubes and pop it in the microwave for a few seconds.

2 eggs
1 stick (4 ounces) softened unsalted butter
1 cup sugar
2 cups self-rising flour
⅔ cup milk
1 teaspoon vanilla extract

Preheat the oven to 350°F. Lightly grease an 8" round cake pan.

Combine all ingredients into a large bowl, using an electric mixer at the low speed for 60 seconds or until combined.

Scrape down the sides and then mix at high for 2 minutes, until the mixture is thick.

Pour mixture into pan and bake for 30–45 minutes until the cake is golden and a toothpick inserted into the middle comes out clean.

Allow to cool in pan for 5 minutes before turning out on a rack to cool. Allow the cake to cool completely before you start crumbling to make the cake pops as the steamy hot cake mixture could burn little hands.

BE SURE TO REMOVE THE BROWN CRUST PRIOR TO CRUMBLING THE CAKE.

Quick and Easy Chocolate Cake

This recipe will yield 25 pops with the addition of ¾ cup of frosting and 18 ounces of candy coating for dipping.

1 cup self-rising flour

¼ cup unsweetened cocoa

½ cup sugar

2 sticks (8 ounces) unsalted butter, melted and cooled

2 large eggs at room temperature

1 teaspoon vanilla extract

1. Preheat the oven to 325°F. Grease an 8" round cake pan and line the bottom with parchment paper.
2. Sift together flour, cocoa, and sugar in a large bowl. Add the melted butter, eggs, and vanilla and mix with a handheld mixer at low speed until just combined. Increase speed to high and mix for 2 minutes. The mixture will lighten and become thick.
3. Pour the mixture into the prepared pan and bake for 25–30 minutes or until a skewer inserted into the middle comes out clean.

POP TIP

ADD A LITTLE WHOLESOME GOODNESS AND REPLACE 1 CUP OF THE SELF-RISING FLOUR WITH WHOLE WHEAT SELF-RISING FLOUR. AFTER SIFTING, MAKE SURE TO POP ALL THE HUSKS BACK INTO THE MIX. THE KIDS WON'T NOTICE THE TASTE OR TEXTURE IN THE FINISHED POPS.

Special Cake Flavors and Variations

You don't have to stick to just plain vanilla and chocolate. If your favorite flavor is strawberry or pumpkin spice, choose that as your base!

Strawberry Cake

This recipe will yield 30 pops with the addition of ¾ cup Raspberry Buttercream (see Chapter 9) and 18 ounces candy coating for dipping.

Make dainty pretty pink cake balls with this delicious fruity recipe.

1 stick (4 ounces) unsalted butter at room temperature

½ cup sugar

2 eggs

1 teaspoon vanilla extract

1 teaspoon strawberry extract (optional)

A few drops red liquid food color (optional)

2 cups self-rising flour, sifted

½ cup milk

½ cup fresh strawberries, puréed

1. Preheat oven to 325°F and line an 8" round cake pan with parchment paper.
2. In a large bowl cream butter and sugar at high speed until light and fluffy. Reduce speed to medium low and add the eggs one a time, mixing until combined. Add the vanilla, strawberry extract, and food color and mix well.
3. Reduce speed to low and add one cup of the flour, mixing until just combined. Add the milk and mix, scraping down the sides of the bowl as required to combine the ingredients. Mix in the remaining flour.
4. Fold in the strawberries and pour mixture into the prepared pan.
5. Bake for 40–45 minutes until a skewer comes out clean. Cool in pan.

Pumpkin Spice Cake

This recipe will yield 20 pops with the addition of ¾ to 1 cup frosting and 18 ounces candy coating for dipping.

A deliciously moist and fragrantly spicy cake, perfect for when you want to make something enticingly different.

2 cups all-purpose flour

¼ teaspoon baking powder

3 teaspoons pumpkin pie spice mix

½ teaspoon salt

1 stick (4 ounces) unsalted butter at room temperature

1¼ cups light brown sugar, lightly packed

2 large eggs at room temperature

1 cup puréed pumpkin (canned or fresh)

1 teaspoon vanilla extract

½ cup buttermilk

1. Preheat oven to 350°F. Grease and flour an 8" round cake pan.
2. In a large bowl sift together the flour, baking powder, pie spice, and salt. Set aside.
3. In the bowl of an electric mixer, mix together butter and sugar at medium high until fluffy. Reduce speed to medium low and add the eggs one at a time, scraping down the sides of the bowl as required to combine the ingredients between additions. Add the pumpkin and vanilla and mix until just combined.
4. Reduce speed to low and add half the flour mixture just until combined; do not overmix. Add the buttermilk and then the remaining flour mixture. Scrap down the sides of the bowl as required to combine.
5. Pour the mixture into the prepared pan and bake for 25–30 minutes or until a skewer inserted into the middle comes out clean. Allow to cool in pan for 5 minutes before turning out on a rack to cool completely.

Moo-Free Cake

This recipe will yield 24 pops with the addition of ½ cup frosting and 18 ounces of candy coating for dipping.

Just because you can't have dairy, doesn't mean you have to miss out on the fun of eating cake pops! This cake recipe is perfect for those who are lactose intolerant, and it can be used in place of any of the cake bases.

1½ cups self-rising flour

¼ cup unsweetened cocoa

1 cup sugar

¼ cup + 2 tablespoons vegetable oil

1 teaspoon vanilla

1 teaspoon vinegar

1 cup water

1. Preheat oven to 375°F. Grease an 8" round cake pan and line the bottom with parchment paper.
2. Sift flour and cocoa together. Add sugar, oil, vanilla, and vinegar. Pour water over all the ingredients and mix well with a fork or whisk until smooth.
3. Bake for 20–25 minutes.

This recipe will yield 25 pops with the addition of 18 ounces of candy coating for dipping (no frosting required).

Gluten free doesn't mean fun free, so you don't have to be left out of the cake pop revolution! This cake is so moist and rich there is no need to add frosting; just scrunch and crumble the whole cake.

> 1¾ cups semisweet chocolate chips
> 2 sticks minus 2 tablespoons (7 ounces) unsalted butter
> 4 eggs, separated
> 1 cup sugar
> 1 teaspoon vanilla extract

1. Preheat oven to 325°F. Line the bottom and sides of a 9" cake pan with parchment paper.
2. Melt the chocolate and the butter in the microwave on medium-low heat for bursts of 60 seconds each, stirring in between each burst, for a total of approximately 4 minutes. Do not overheat.
3. In a large bowl mix together the egg yolks and ½ cup of sugar with an electric mixer at medium-high speed for around 3 minutes, until fluffy and very light in color. Reduce speed to medium low and mix in the melted chocolate mixture and the vanilla.
4. In a clean bowl with clean mixer attachments, beat the egg whites at high speed until stiff and foamy. Add the remaining ½ cup sugar gradually and mix well.
5. Fold ¼ of the egg-white mixture into the egg yolk and chocolate mixture. Once combined, lightly fold in the remaining egg whites.
6. Bake for 1 hour and 15 minutes or until a skewer inserted into the middle comes out mostly clean with a few crumbs. Start to check after 1 hour.
7. When the cake has cooled, crumble it into a large bowl. The outside will be very crusty and require a lot of crumbling, and the inside will be gooey. Mix it all together, form cake balls using 4 teaspoons of mixture place on a tray lined with parchment paper. Pop into the fridge to chill for around an hour before proceeding with any of the cake pop variations.

POP TIP

WHEN DECORATING, CHECK THE INGREDIENTS AND ADDITIVES OF ALL THE CANDY YOU ARE USING TO MAKE SURE IT IS GLUTEN FREE; THERE IS A WIDE VARIETY OF GLUTEN-FREE SUBSTITUTES AVAILABLE AT BOTH GROCERY AND SPECIALTY STORES. AT THE TIME OF PRINTING, WILTON CANDY COATING WAS GLUTEN FREE.

This recipe will yield 28 pops with the addition of 1 cup cream cheese frosting and 18 ounces candy coating for dipping.

Red Velvet Cake makes a super cake pop base, because the surprise of biting into the unexpected rich color is a treat in itself. Make sure everyone wears aprons to protect their clothes from the red food color.

2 tablespoons red food color (liquid, not gel)

1 tablespoon unsweetened cocoa powder

1 teaspoon vanilla extract

1½ cups all-purpose flour

½ teaspoon salt

1 teaspoon baking powder

½ teaspoon baking soda

1 stick (4 ounces) unsalted butter at room temperature

¾ cup sugar

1 egg at room temperature

½ cup buttermilk

1. Preheat oven to 325°F and line an 8" round cake pan with parchment paper.
2. In a small bowl mix the food color, cocoa powder, and vanilla together to make a paste. In a large bowl sift together the flour, salt, baking powder, and baking soda. Set aside.
3. In a large bowl cream the butter and sugar at high speed until light and fluffy, around 3 minutes. Reduce speed to medium low and add the egg. Mix until combined. Add the cocoa mixture and mix well.
4. Reduce speed to low and add half the flour mixture, mixing until just combined. Add the buttermilk, scraping down the sides of the bowl as required to mix the ingredients. Add the remaining flour mixture; combine.
5. Bake for 30–35 minutes until a skewer inserted into the middle comes out clean. Cool in pan.

IF YOU ONLY HAVE GEL FOOD COLOR, USE ½ TO ¾ TEASPOON PLUS ENOUGH WARM WATER TO EQUAL A TOTAL OF 2 TABLESPOONS.

This recipe will yield 20 pops with the addition of 18 ounces candy coating for dipping (no frosting required).

Since this cake is already creamy, no frosting is needed to turn it into cake pops. Just dip the cheesecake balls into the candy coating and you have a treat that's hard to beat. For a kid-friendly way to line the springform pan, tear off a square of parchment paper slightly larger than the pan, lay it over the bottom section of the pan, then close the springform sides around it. The corners of the paper should hang out, which will also make it easier to slide the cake off the bottom when you need to. If you don't have a springform pan, just use a regular cake pan and scoop the mixture straight out of the pan once the cheesecake has cooled.

> 24 ounces (three 8-ounce packages) cream cheese at room temperature
>
> 1 tablespoon all-purpose flour
>
> 1 tablespoon lemon juice
>
> 1 teaspoon vanilla extract
>
> 2 eggs at room temperature

1. Preheat oven to 325°F and line a 9" springform baking pan with parchment paper.
2. Beat cream cheese until light and fluffy. Reduce speed to low, add the flour, lemon juice, and vanilla, and mix for 60 seconds. Add the eggs one at a time and mix until well combined.
3. Pour the mixture into the prepared pan and bake for 1 hour and 15 minutes. If the top starts to brown too early, turn down the temperature by 10 degrees.
4. Allow to cool and then place in the fridge to chill.
5. Once chilled, remove from the fridge, undo the top of the springform pan, and slide the cheesecake off the base of the pan. Scoop out the creamy center and roll into balls using 4 teaspoons of mixture for each ball. Leave any brown edges around the cheesecake and discard them. Wash hands in water as required; if they become sticky it will be more difficult to roll the balls.

IF YOU REALLY CAN'T DO WITHOUT THE TASTE OF CRUNCHY GRAHAM CRACKERS WITH CHEESECAKE, CRUMBLE 5 OR SO CRACKERS INTO SMALL PIECES AND SPRINKLE OVER THE CANDY COATING AFTER YOU HAVE DIPPED THE CAKE BALLS.

FROSTING

While cake is the first ingredient in delicious cake pops, frosting is the second—and the most important. Frosting is what makes the cake balls stick together so you can dip and decorate them. Here are two recipes for basic frosting—vanilla buttercream and chocolate buttercream. Check out Chapter 9 for more variations on frosting.

Vanilla Buttercream Frosting

Makes 2 cups (approximately 16 ounces)

This classic, sweet, and simple frosting, often used as icing for cake or cupcakes, is also perfect for cake pops. In very warm weather the milk may not be required, so mix the other ingredients and add at the end if needed.

- 1 stick (4 ounces) unsalted butter at room temperature
- 3 cups powdered sugar, sifted
- 2 tablespoons milk
- 1 teaspoon vanilla extract

1. In the bowl of an electric mixer, combine all the ingredients at low speed. Increase to high speed and continue mixing for 3 minutes or until the frosting is light and fluffy.

SUBSTITUTE DAIRY-FREE SPREAD FOR THE BUTTER AND LEAVE OUT THE MILK FOR A DAIRY-FREE VERSION TO USE IN CAKE POP MIXTURES.

Chocolate Buttercream Frosting

Makes 2 cups

Rich buttercream frosting made with cocoa instead of baking chocolate means no messy melting and easy one-bowl mixing. This frosting is perfect for icing cupcakes, decorating cookies, and adding to cake pop mixtures.

- 1 stick (4 ounces) unsalted butter at room temperature
- 1 cup unsweetened cocoa
- 2 cups powdered sugar, sifted
- ¼ cup milk
- 1 teaspoon vanilla extract

1. In the bowl of an electric mixer, combine all the ingredients at low speed. Increase mixer to high speed and continue mixing for 3 minutes or until the frosting is fluffy.

Assembling the Cake Pops

Once you have your cake and frosting, you're ready to begin the cake pop creativity.

Crumble the cake into very fine pieces with your hands into a large wide shallow pan. Rake your fingers through to find any large pieces left and crumble them up as well. Show the kids how to do this and then let them finish the job.

Add the suggested amount of frosting as listed in each cake recipe. Scrunch the frosting in with your hands until the mixture is evenly distributed and holds together easily when you press it together. If the mixture is too dry, it will not hold together properly and crumble; if it is too wet, then the balls will not be able to hold their shape. In the Cake Pop Variations section later in this chapter, some of the recipes call for "cake pop mixture." The cake combined with the frosting is what this refers to. Unless specified otherwise in a recipe, you can use any cake and frosting combination you like for your cake pop variations.

Shaping the Pops

Once you have the mixture at the correct consistency, it's time to shape the cake balls.

There are two different methods: hand rolling and pressing the mixture into small cookie or fondant cutters. Before beginning either method, line a tray with parchment paper to hold the shaped cake balls.

To hand-roll the mixture, measure out 4 teaspoons, which should make a round of around 1½" in diameter. Scrunch the mixture together lightly in your hand and then roll it between your palms to make the ball as smooth as you can. The rolled ball should be firmly packed so it will hold its shape. Using light pressure when rolling will be sufficient; you will not need to press your hands together very hard.

The ball is a good starting point for making other shapes. If you need an oval, just manipulate the shape by rolling your palms back and forth a little. A teardrop shape can be made by pinching one end and lightly flattening the sides. Once the cake ball is shaped the way you want it, place it on the tray lined with parchment paper.

To make the cake ball shapes using the pressing method, place the shaped cutter on the tray lined with parchment paper and press about 2 tablespoons of mixture into the shape. Turn the cutter over to see if the underneath is smooth, with no holes or gaps. If there are holes, turn the shape over again and press the mixture down firmer.

Once you are happy that the underneath is smooth, use your thumb to lightly press out the mixture onto the parchment-lined tray, being careful not to break the shape. Once you have released the mixture, turn it over so the smooth side is on the top and then gently press down on the shaped cake mixture. This should help to flatten the other side.

When all of the mixture is shaped to your satisfaction, pop the tray into the fridge and chill for around an hour.

Dipping in Candy and Attaching Lollipop Sticks

Once you've made the cake balls, it's time to dip them in candy coating and attach the lollipop stick. Candy coating or melts are called for in most of the recipes in this book as they are more stable and easier to use than regular chocolate in this situation.

Melt your candy coating in the microwave on medium low at short bursts of 60–90 seconds. This might seem like a lot of work, but the coating can be very delicate and overheating will ruin a whole batch. If you prefer, you can use a double boiler on the stovetop, but that involves a lot of extra cleaning up and is not so safe for the kiddies. If using the stovetop, always use a double boiler; never use a saucepan directly on the heat.

If you're using a block of coating, cut or break it into small pieces before melting. Candy melts or buttons are good to go as they are.

Use a clean, dry, microwave-safe dish for melting and a clean, dry, metal spoon for stirring. Wooden spoons may have a little moisture in them, and you really don't want to get any water in with your candy coating. Water will seize the coating, making it unusable for dipping.

Candy Coating Consistency

One of the most important things about dipping pops and other sweets on a stick is the consistency of the melted candy coating. Most brands, when melted, will be just a little too thick for a really smooth finish. Add some paramount crystals or vegetable shortening (like Crisco) when you melt the candy coating. The amount required will vary depending on the brand of candy coating you use. Start off with around 1 ounce of crystals per 14 ounces of candy coating during the melting process and add more as required until the mixture is fluid enough for dipping.

Securing the Stick

Is there anything worse than dipping a treat and losing the whole thing in the bowl of melted candy coating? Well, maybe, but with this simple trick the chances of it happening will be minimal.

Here's the secret: Make sure you dip the end of the lollipop stick in a little melted candy coating before you insert it into the cake pops, marshmallows, cupcakes, or other treats. Then pop them into the fridge to set for 10 minutes before continuing with the coating. How easy is that? It's like a yummy glue.

Dipping and Getting a Smooth Finish

Okay, you have your coating at the right consistency, the sticks are secured . . . time to start dipping.

Make sure your dipping bowl is deep enough for the candy coating to cover the whole pop. Dip the pop and then lift it out of the melted candy. Holding the pop over the bowl to catch drips, gently tap the stick against your hand or the side of the bowl to remove excess candy coating. Remove as much excess as possible before you put the pop into the Styrofoam block to set.

As you work, remember that not every pop will be perfect, especially with kids helping. Have fun, relax, and just put any especially wonky ones at the back of the display.

Oh No, a Crack!

Sometimes after you have finished making cake pops you will notice a crack. Don't despair. To fix this problem, remelt a small amount of the leftover candy coating and, using a toothpick, fill in the crack with the melted candy. Then run a gloved or clean finger along the crack to smooth away the excess. It won't be completely perfect, but you will have to look closely to know there was a problem.

Leftover Candy Coating

When dipping, you will always need to melt more candy coating than you are going to use; if you didn't, there would not be enough to dip all of each pop or treat into the bowl.

Carefully pour any leftover candy coating onto greaseproof paper, let it set, and then store it in a Ziploc bag until you need it again. Then you can just break it up and pop it into your microwave-safe bowl, ready to melt.

Cake Pop Storage

Once decorated and set, cake pops should be stored in an airtight container in the fridge for up to 3 days. Undecorated cake ball mixture can be frozen wrapped in plastic wrap and sealed in an airtight container for 4 weeks. When ready to use, completely defrost in the fridge still in the airtight container.

CAKE POP VARIATIONS

As soon as the coating has set, it's ready to be decorated! Here you'll find a bunch of variations of cake pops sure to delight kids and adults alike. Feel free to get creative and come up with new decorating methods. Ask your kids what they think the best decorations would be. This is about having fun with your kids—not about being perfect.

❖ ❖ ❖

Peanut Butter Chocolate Nirvana Pops

Peanut butter and chocolate are made for each other. Combining them in a cake pop takes this favorite flavor fusion to another blissful level.

1 Quick and Easy Chocolate Cake
¾ cup Peanut Butter Frosting (see Chapter 9)
2 tablespoons smooth peanut butter
18 ounces chocolate candy coating

1. Line a tray with parchment paper.
2. Follow the basic pop recipe, adding in the peanut butter with the frosting. Shape into balls, place on the parchment-lined tray, and pop into the fridge for an hour to chill.
3. Melt the candy coating as described in the Melting Tips section earlier in this chapter. Dip the end of each stick into the melted candy and push one stick into each of the cake pop balls. Return to parchment-lined tray and pop back into the fridge to chill for 10 minutes.
4. Remelt the candy coating if necessary. Remove tray from fridge. Holding the end of the stick, dip each cake pop into the melted candy until the whole round is submerged, and then lift it out of the melted candy. Holding the pop over the bowl to catch drips, gently tap the stick against your hand or the side of the bowl to remove excess candy coating. Remove as much excess as possible before you put the pop into the Styrofoam block to set.

Coconut Ice Cake Pops

A fusion of cake and candy, this recipe combines the best of both treats and then sticks it on a pop. Brilliant!

1 Quick and Easy Vanilla Cake

1 cup shredded coconut, plus 3 tablespoons for decorating

½ cup condensed milk

18 ounces white candy coating

7 ounces pink candy coating

1. Line a tray with parchment paper.
2. Remove the hard crusts from the vanilla cake and crumble it into fine crumbs. Add 1 cup shredded coconut and the condensed milk and mix until well combined. Shape into balls, place on the parchment-lined tray, and pop into the fridge to chill for an hour.
3. Melt the white candy coating as described in the Melting Tips section earlier in this chapter. Dip the end of each stick into the melted candy and push one stick into each of the cake pop balls. Return to parchment-lined tray and pop back into the fridge to chill for 10 minutes.
4. Remelt the white candy coating if necessary. Remove tray from fridge. Holding the end of the stick, dip a cake pop into the melted candy until the whole round is submerged, and then lift it out of the melted candy. Holding the pop over the bowl to catch drips, gently tap the stick against your hand or the side of the bowl to remove excess candy coating. Remove as much excess as possible before you put the pop into the Styrofoam block to set.
5. Melt the pink candy coating and dip one of the white-candy-dipped cake pops in, only submerging the top half. You want the end result to look like half white and half pink coconut ice. Continue to hold upside down to allow all excess candy coating to drip away. Place upright into the Styrofoam block and quickly sprinkle on a little extra coconut.
6. Repeat for remaining pops and leave to set.

Coconut Ice
Cake Pops

Gumball Pops

If you love the look of gumball machines but don't love the kids chewing gum, this sweet on a stick is a cute compromise. Little kids just love shaking on the sprinkles.

1 batch cake pop mixture (any flavor)
18 ounces white candy coating
Confetti sprinkles
Froot Loops cereal

1. Line a tray with parchment paper.
2. Shape the cake pop mixture into ovals and place shapes onto the parchment-lined tray. Chill until firm.
3. Prepare the Froot Loops for use in the recipe later by gently pushing a lollipop stick through the hole of each piece of cereal, making the inside hole a little bigger and easier to slide on the lollipop stick.
4. Melt the candy coating as described in the Melting Tips section earlier in this chapter. Dip the end of each stick into the melted candy and push one stick into the bottom of each oval shape. Return to parchment-lined tray and pop back into the fridge to chill for 10 minutes.
5. Remelt the candy coating if necessary. Remove tray from fridge. Holding the end of the stick, dip a cake pop into the melted candy until the whole shape is submerged, and then lift it out of the melted candy. Holding the pop over the bowl to catch drips, gently tap the stick against your hand or the side of the bowl to remove excess candy coating. Remove as much excess as possible.
6. Holding the pop upside down (stick upward), slip a piece of Froot Loops cereal onto the lollipop stick. Push the cereal down the stick to touch the coating on the bottom of the cake pop. Quickly shake the confetti sprinkles around the bottom two-thirds of the cake pop to resemble gum in a machine.
7. Place the pop upright into the Styrofoam block and place another piece of Froot Loops cereal onto the top of the pop.
8. Repeat for remaining pops and leave to set.

Gumball Pops

◆◆◆

Crazy Car Pops

Vroom vroom! The kids will be zooming around honking and tooting for you to get out of the way once they have these cool cars in their hot little hands. Make Traffic Light Cookies (Chapter 4) at the same time for complementary treats.

1 batch cake pop mixture (any flavor)
18 ounces red candy coating
Brown Reese's Pieces
Yellow confetti sprinkles
Mini Tootsie Fruit Rolls

1. Line a tray with parchment paper.
2. Make cake pop mixture into a half-circle shape, with slightly flat sides. If you like, press down on the front and back to make a shape like a toy car. Place shapes onto the parchment-lined tray and chill until firm.
3. Melt the candy coating as described in the Melting Tips section earlier in this chapter. Dip the end of each stick into the melted candy and push one stick into the bottom flat/underneath side of each of the car cake pop shapes. Return to parchment-lined tray and pop back into the fridge to chill for 10 minutes.
4. Remelt the candy coating if necessary. Remove tray from fridge. Holding the end of the stick, dip each cake pop into the melted candy until the whole shape is submerged, and then lift it out of the melted candy. Holding the pop over the bowl to catch drips, gently tap the stick against your hand or the side of the bowl to remove excess candy coating. Remove as much excess as possible before you put the pop into the Styrofoam block to set. Repeat for remaining mixture.
5. Using your fingers or a small rolling pin, flatten out a Tootsie Roll as thin as you can ⅛" or thinner. Cut off a small rectangle to look like a windshield. Use a small amount of melted candy as "glue" to stick the Tootsie Roll windshield onto a cake pop. Repeat for all the pops.
6. Use a small amount of the melted candy to adhere the Reese's Pieces to the side of each cake pop to look like wheels.
7. With a little melted candy, adhere 2 confetti sprinkles to the front of each car pop to look like headlights. Allow pops to set.

Spotty Dotty Polka Pops

The trick to making these lip-smacking M&M's-filled chocolate treats is to make a hole for the lollipop stick right at the start. If you don't, all those hidden chocolate treats might impede your progress later.

1 batch chocolate cake pop mixture
1 cup M&M's Minis, plus extra for decorating
18 ounces candy coating

1. Line a tray with parchment paper.
2. Mix the M&M's Minis into the chocolate cake pop mix until well combined. Shape into balls and place on the parchment-lined tray.
3. Use a lollipop stick to make a hole in each ball where you intend to insert the stick later. If you are unable to push the stick through any of the balls because of the M&M's, you may need to roll them again. Pop the tray into the fridge to chill for an hour.
4. Melt the candy coating as described in the Melting Tips section earlier in this chapter. Dip the end of each stick into the candy and push into the premade holes. Return the cake pops to the parchment-lined tray and pop back into the fridge to chill for 10 minutes.
5. Remelt the candy coating if necessary. Remove tray from fridge. Holding the end of the stick, dip a cake pop into the melted candy until the whole round is submerged, and then lift it out of the melted candy. Holding the pop over the bowl to catch drips, gently tap the stick against your hand or the side of the bowl to remove excess candy coating. Remove as much excess as possible

before you put the pop into the Styrofoam block. Quickly top with one M&M's candy.
6. Repeat for remaining pops and leave to set.

Abominable Snowman Pops

Just too sweet to be scary, these pops start off looking like a sugary snowball and end up as lovable monsters.

1 batch vanilla cake pop mixture
Black edible marker
Blue confetti sprinkles
18 ounces white candy coating
White nonpareil sprinkles

1. Line a tray with parchment paper.
2. Make cake pop mixture into round shapes. Place shapes onto the parchment-lined tray and chill until firm.
3. Use the edible marker to draw an eye onto each of the confetti sprinkles.
4. Melt the candy coating as described in the Melting Tips section earlier in this chapter. Dip the end of each stick into the melted candy and push one stick into each of the cake pop balls. Return to parchment-lined tray and pop back into the fridge to chill for 10 minutes.
5. Remelt the candy coating if necessary. Remove tray from fridge. Holding the end of the stick, dip a cake pop into the melted candy until the whole round is submerged,

and then lift it out of the melted candy. Holding the pop over the bowl to catch drips, gently tap the stick against your hand or the side of the bowl to remove excess candy coating. Remove as much excess as possible.

6. Working quickly, use the end of a spoon to tap all over the pop to make the candy coating rough. Sprinkle entire pop lightly with the white nonpareils.

7. Put the confetti sprinkles on the front of the pop to resemble eyes and then place the pop into the Styrofoam block.

8. Repeat for remaining pops and leave to set.

POP TIP

TO MAKE MRS. ABOMINABLE SNOWMAN, USE PINK CONFETTI SPRINKLES IN PLACE OF THE BLUE AND ADD TWO HEART SPRINKLES JOINED TOGETHER WITH MELTED CANDY COATING AT THE POINTED END TO RESEMBLE A HAIR BOW.

Abominable Snowman Pops

Funfetti Pops

Little mouthfuls of multicolored sweet joy on a stick await you when you make up these fun little treats.

1 batch vanilla cake pop mixture
½ cup confetti sprinkles, plus extra for decorating
18 ounces white candy coating

1. Line a tray with parchment paper.
2. Mix the confetti sprinkles into the vanilla cake pop mixture until well combined. Shape the mixture into balls, place on the parchment-lined tray, and pop into the fridge for an hour to chill.
3. Melt the candy coating as described in the Melting Tips section earlier in this chapter. Dip the end of each stick into the melted candy and push one stick into each of the cake pop balls. Return to parchment-lined tray and pop back into the fridge to chill for 10 minutes.
4. Remelt the candy coating if necessary. Remove tray from fridge. Holding the end of the stick, dip a cake pop into the melted candy until the whole round is submerged, and then lift it out of the melted candy. Holding the pop over the bowl to catch drips, gently tap the stick against your hand or the side of the bowl to remove excess candy coating. Remove as much excess as possible before you put the pop into the Styrofoam block to set. Quickly top with confetti sprinkles.
5. Repeat for remaining pops and leave to set.

Nutty About You Pops

Use your favorite type of nuts on these pops or mix a few together to make a totally nutalicious treat.

1 batch chocolate cake pop mixture
18 ounces chocolate candy coating
Crushed nuts

1. Line a tray with parchment paper.
2. Shape cake pop mixture into balls. Place on the parchment-lined tray and chill until firm.
3. Melt the candy coating as described in the Melting Tips section earlier in this chapter. Dip the end of each stick into the melted candy and push one stick into each of the cake pop balls. Return to parchment-lined tray and pop back into the fridge to chill for 10 minutes.
4. Remelt the candy coating if necessary. Remove tray from fridge. Holding the end of the stick, dip a cake pop into the melted candy until the whole round is submerged, and then lift it out of the melted candy. Holding the pop over the bowl to catch drips, gently tap the stick against your hand or the side of the bowl to remove excess candy coating. Remove as much excess as possible before you put the pop into the Styrofoam block to set. Quickly sprinkle the crushed nuts over the pop.
5. Repeat for remaining pops and leave to set.

You can be sure no one will be as slow as a snail when it comes to helping to decorate and munch on these tasty garden pests. The shells will look cute in other colors like light green and pink if you prefer.

1 batch cake pop mixture (any flavor)

18 ounces peanut butter candy coating

Peanut butter Whoppers

½ cup brown Royal Icing (see Chapter 9)

Small round cookie cutter (about 1¾")

1. Line a tray with parchment paper.
2. Press the cake pop mixture into the round cookie cutter, using the pressing method described in Shaping the Pops earlier in this chapter. Lay the shapes down flat on the parchment-lined tray.
3. Use a knife to cut a straight line through each pop to make a flat bottom in the circle about ½" from the edge Don't discard the section you cut off. The mixture you remove from the bottom can be reused to make more cake pops. The shape of the pop should now look similar to a snail shell. Place the tray into the fridge and chill until firm, around 10 minutes.
4. Melt the candy coating, dip the end of each stick into the melted candy, and push the stick into the flat bottom edge of the disk on each of the cake pops. Return to parchment-lined tray and pop back into fridge to chill for 10 minutes.
5. Remelt the candy coating if necessary. Remove tray from fridge. Holding the end of the stick, dip each cake pop into the melted candy until the whole shape is submerged, and then lift it out of the melted candy. Holding the pop over the bowl to catch drips, gently tap the stick against your hand or the side of the bowl to remove excess candy coating. Remove as much excess as possible before you put the pop into the Styrofoam block. Repeat for remaining mixture and allow to set.
6. Cut a small slice off each of the Whoppers to make a flat section on one side. Using a little of the melted candy as "glue," adhere the flat side of each of the Whoppers to a "shell" pop, on the outside edge of circle, so it looks like a snail head peeking out of its shell.
7. Put the brown Royal Icing into a Ziploc bag and cut a very small hole in the corner. Pipe a swirl on the flat edge of the pop to look like the snail shell swirl. Pipe one side of each pop and allow to set before piping the swirl on the other side.
8. Once both sides are set, pipe a couple of Royal Icing eyes on each of the Whoppers "heads."

BETWEEN USES, KEEP THE ZIPLOC BAG OF ROYAL ICING IN AN AIRTIGHT CONTAINER WITH A PIECE OF DAMP PAPER TOWEL COVERING THE HOLE TO PREVENT IT FROM DRYING OUT.

Big Mouth Monster Pops

To get the scary open monster mouth you will need to use a different dipping technique, but the results are so scarily fun that learning this trick is worth it.

1 batch Red Velvet or Strawberry Cake pop mixture
18 ounces blue candy coating
Mini marshmallows
Packet of ready-made mini sugar eyes

1. Line a cookie sheet with parchment paper. Prepare more parchment paper for making monster mouths: Cut out twenty-four 1" × 1" pieces of parchment paper and fold each in half to make folded rectangles 1" × ½".
2. Using safety scissors, cut the marshmallows into quarters, and then roll the quarters between your fingers to make the ends pointy, so they look like little monster fangs.
3. Shape cake pop mixture into balls. Place on tray covered with parchment paper and chill until firm.
4. Melt the candy coating as described in the Melting Tips section earlier in this chapter. Dip the end of each stick into the melted candy and push one stick into each of the cake pop balls. Return to parchment-lined tray and pop back into the fridge to chill for 10 minutes.
5. When the stick is secured, use a knife to cut a line across the front bottom of the round where you would like the mouth to be. Insert a piece of the folded parchment paper into the cut with the V of the fold pointing into the pop. You will be pulling this paper out after dipping to make an open mouth.

Big Mouth Monster Pops

6. Remelt the candy coating if necessary. Hold a pop over the top of the bowl and spoon the coating over the whole pop, being careful around the parchment paper area so it doesn't fill in with coating. You are looking for a messy finish, so if the spooning technique does not leave the candy coating looking bumpy enough, pat it all over with the back of the spoon to make little peaks.

7. Holding the pop, allow the coating to harden for just a few seconds (do not allow it to set) and then pull out the parchment paper to expose the open mouth. If the melted candy smudges into the mouth, use the end of a spoon or lollipop stick to scrape out any candy so you can see the red cake inside.

8. Place the pop in the Styrofoam block. Working quickly, put 2 marshmallow fangs on the bottom of the mouth and 2 on the top. Add 1 to 3 eyes toward the top of the round.

9. Repeat for remaining mixture and leave to set.

Alien Invasion Pops

Eeek, it's an alien invasion! Get the kids to help create these pops and then save the planet from them by demolishing them as quickly as they can.

1 batch cake pop mixture (any flavor)
18 ounces light green candy coating
Brown Reese's Pieces
Black edible marker (optional)

1. Line a tray with parchment paper.

2. Make cake pop mixture into oval shapes. If you like, you can make the bottom a little bit thinner to resemble a chin. Place shapes onto parchment-lined tray and chill until firm.

3. Melt the candy coating as described in the Melting Tips section earlier in this chapter. Dip the end of each stick into the melted candy and push one stick into each of the oval shapes. Return to parchment-lined tray and pop back into the fridge to chill for 10 minutes.

4. Remelt the candy coating if necessary. Remove tray from fridge. Holding the end of the stick, dip a cake pop into the melted candy until the whole shape is submerged, and then lift it out of the melted candy. Holding the pop over the bowl to catch drips, gently tap the stick against your hand or the side of the bowl to remove excess candy coating. Remove as much excess as possible before you put the pop into the Styrofoam block to set.

5. When pops are set, remelt a little of the left over melted green candy coating to stick 2 brown Reese's Pieces near the top of each so they look like large alien eyes. Hold a moment until they are secured.

6. Once the candy coating is completely dry, you can use an edible marker to draw on a mouth.

St. Patrick's Day Shamrocks

Bring a little luck your way with these cheerful shamrock pops. If you have trouble finding a shamrock cutter, make round cake pops, dip them in white candy coating, and decorate with shamrock sprinkles.

1 batch Green Velvet Cake pop mix (see sidebar)
18 ounces dark green candy coating
Small (1½") shamrock cookie cuter

1. Line a couple of trays with parchment paper.
2. Press the cake pop mixture into the shamrock cookie cutter, using the pressing method described in Shaping the Pops earlier in this chapter. Spend a bit of time getting the shapes flat on the top, as holes will show in the end result. Lay the shapes down flat on the parchment-lined tray.
3. Melt the green candy coating as described in the Melting Tips section earlier in this chapter. Dip the end of each stick into the melted candy and then, leaving the shamrocks lying flat on the tray, insert one stick into the stem of each shape.
4. Leaving the shapes lying down flat, place the tray into the fridge to firm up for 10 minutes.
5. Remelt the candy coating if necessary. Remove tray from fridge. Holding the end of the stick, dip each cake pop into the melted candy until the whole shape is submerged, and then lift it out of the melted candy. Holding the pop over the bowl to catch drips, gently tap the stick against your hand or the side of the bowl to remove excess candy coating. Remove as much excess as possible before you put the pop into the Styrofoam block to set.
6. Repeat for remaining pops and leave to set.

POP TIP

FOR GREEN VELVET CAKE, MAKE UP A BATCH OF RED VELVET CAKE BUT USE 2 TABLESPOONS OF LIQUID GREEN FOOD COLOR IN PLACE OF THE RED.

◆ ◆ ◆

Bunch of Roses

A pretty bunch of roses that you can eat as well, just perfect for Valentine's Day or Mother's Day. Serve a bunch of these in a pretty cup filled with pink and white candy and they will look like a beautiful bouquet.

1 batch cake pop mixture (any flavor)
18 ounces red candy coating

1. Line a tray with parchment paper.
2. Make cake pop mixture into oval shapes. Place shapes onto parchment-lined tray and chill until firm.
3. Melt the candy coating as described in the Melting Tips section earlier in this chapter. Dip the end of each stick into the melted candy and push one stick into each of the oval shapes. Return to parchment-lined tray and pop back into the fridge to chill for 10 minutes.

4. Remelt the candy coating if necessary. Remove tray from fridge. Holding the end of the stick, dip a cake pop into the melted candy until the whole round is submerged, and then lift it out of the melted candy. Holding the pop over the bowl to catch drips, gently tap the stick against your hand or the side of the bowl to remove excess candy coating. Remove as much excess as possible before you put the pop into the Styrofoam block to set. Repeat for remaining pops.

5. Pour some of the remaining candy coating into a Ziploc or piping bag with a small hole cut in the corner. Working very quickly, before the candy hardens and blocks the hole, pipe swirls on the top of each pop, starting in the middle and working out to the edge. If the candy mixture hardens, you will need to remelt it. If you have a hot water bottle, you can try laying the bag on top of it and squishing the mixture around until smooth, or you can just melt more candy coating and use a new Ziploc bag.

USE PINK, WHITE, OR YELLOW CANDY COATING, OR EVEN A MIXTURE, TO MATCH YOUR BOUQUET TO THE OCCASION.

Bunch of Roses

POPZ!

These are pops in the truest sense. The kids will adore sprinkling on the Pop Rocks and the anticipation of having them burst in their mouths when they get to eat them. POP!

1 batch chocolate cake pop mixture
18 ounces chocolate candy coating
Pop Rocks candy

1. Line a tray with parchment paper.
2. Shape cake pop mixture into balls. Place on the parchment-lined tray and chill until firm.
3. Melt the candy coating as described in the Melting Tips section earlier in this chapter. Dip the end of each stick into the melted candy and push one stick into each of the cake pop balls. Return to parchment-lined tray and pop back into the fridge to chill for 10 minutes.
4. Remelt the candy coating if necessary. Remove tray from fridge. Holding the end of the stick, dip a cake pop into the melted candy until the whole round is submerged, and then lift it out of the melted candy. Holding the pop over the bowl to catch drips, gently tap the stick against your hand or the side of the bowl to remove excess candy coating. Remove as much excess as possible before you put the pop into the Styrofoam block. Working quickly, sprinkle the Pop Rocks over the pop.
5. Repeat for remaining pops and leave to set.

Pink Princess Pops

These pops are the perfect pinktastic bite-size sweet for any princess-loving little girls. Those who don't love pink can make princely pops by using blue candy coating and sprinkles.

1 batch Quick and Easy Vanilla or Strawberry Cake pop mixture
18 ounces pink candy coating
Pink sprinkles

1. Line a tray with parchment paper.
2. Shape the cake pop mixture into balls. Place onto parchment-lined tray and chill until firm.
3. Melt the pink candy coating as described in the Melting Tips section earlier in this chapter. Dip the end of each stick into the melted candy and push one stick into each of the cake pop balls. Return to parchment-lined tray and pop back into the fridge to chill for 10 minutes.
4. Remelt the candy coating if necessary. Remove tray from fridge. Holding the end of the stick, dip a cake pop into the melted candy until the whole round is submerged, and then lift it out of the melted candy. Holding the pop over the bowl to catch drips, gently tap the stick against your hand or the side of the bowl to remove excess candy coating. Remove as much excess as possible before you put the pop into the Styrofoam block to set. Working quickly, sprinkle the pink sprinkles over the pop.
5. Repeat for remaining pops and leave to set.

Goldfish Bowl Pops

Double-dipped pops that resemble a goldfish bowl—what a super idea! Jelly-type candy fish look great, but any type will do.

1 batch cake pop mixture (any flavor)
18 ounces blue candy coating
9 ounces white candy coating
Fish-shaped candies

1. Line a tray with parchment paper.
2. Make cake pop mixture into round shapes. Place shapes onto parchment-lined tray and chill until firm.
3. Melt the blue candy coating as described in the Melting Tips section earlier in this chapter. Dip the end of each stick into the melted candy and push one stick into the top of each of the cake pop balls. Return to parchment-lined tray and pop back into the fridge to chill for 10 minutes.
4. Remelt the blue candy coating if necessary. Remove tray from fridge. Holding the end of the stick, dip a cake pop into the melted candy until the whole shape is submerged, and then lift it out of the melted candy. Holding the pop over the bowl to catch drips, gently tap the stick against your hand or the side of the bowl to remove most of the excess candy coating, but not quite all. Place each cake pop upside down on the parchment paper (with the top of the pops resting on the paper, sticks upward) to set.
5. Melt the white candy coating and then carefully dip the top of each pop into the melted white candy, only to a depth of about ½". Lift pop out of the melted candy. Holding the pop upside down over the bowl, gently tap the stick on the side of your hand to remove some of the excess candy, but not quite all. Again place the pops upside down onto the parchment paper to set.
6. Once the pops are set, remelt a little of the remaining blue candy and use it to adhere the fish candy onto the blue candy coating on the front of each cake pop. Allow to set.

Goldfish Bowl Pops

Little Blue
Birdhouse
Pops

Sweet
Tweet Bird
Pops

Sweet Tweet Bird Pops

You can make these cute birds in any candy coating color you like; just change the heart sprinkle to a contrasting color. To make the wings for the birds, you will need the candy coating that comes in button melt form.

1 batch cake pop mixture (any flavor)

Jolly Rancher candy chews

24 red candy coating buttons for decoration

18 ounces red candy coating

Blue or pink heart sprinkles

Ready-made sugar eyes or black confetti sprinkles

1. Line a tray with parchment paper.
2. Shape cake pop mixture into balls and pinch one end upward to make a teardrop shape. Flatten the sides.
3. Place the shapes on the parchment-lined tray and pop into the fridge to chill.
4. Cut the Jolly Rancher candy chews into small triangles about ¼" in length. Gently pinch them to make the shape neat.
5. Using a knife, cut 24 candy coating buttons in half. It is easiest to use a sawing motion until you are halfway through the melt and then press down to finish the cut.
6. Melt the candy coating as described in the Melting Tips section earlier in this chapter. Dip the end of each stick into the melted candy and push one stick into each of the cake pop balls. The stick should be inserted in the base of the teardrop shape with the pointed end pointing slightly upward to look like the tail of a bird. Return to parchment-lined tray and pop back into fridge to chill for 10 minutes.

7. Make the wings by using melted candy coating to stick the buttons you have cut into half onto the side of the birds. The candy button halves should be stuck on the body with a pointed tip facing up at about a 45-degree angle. Do the wings on one side of all the pops and then chill in the fridge until set. Turn all the pops over so the side that already has a wing is resting down on the tray and add the remaining cut candy buttons to the upright sides and chill for 10 minutes.
8. Remelt the candy coating if necessary. Remove tray from fridge. Holding the end of the stick, dip a cake pop into the melted candy until the whole shape is submerged, and then lift it out of the melted candy. Holding the pop over the bowl to catch drips, gently tap the stick against your hand or the side of the bowl to remove excess candy coating.
9. Working quickly, before the candy has a chance to set, place a heart sprinkle on the side of each bird where the wing meets the body. Place eyes on each side of the bird at the larger end of the teardrop shape (the head) and then insert the cut Jolly Rancher pieces into the front of the head to look like a beak. Place upright in Styrofoam block.
10. Repeat for remaining pops and leave to set.

This birdhouse just radiates home sweet sugary home. Any square cereal you have handy can be used in place of the cinnamon toast cereal.

> 1 batch cake pop mixture (any flavor)
> ¾" square cookie/fondant cutter
> 18 ounces blue candy coating
> Cinnamon toast breakfast cereal
> Red Pull 'n' Peel Twizzlers cut into ¾" lengths
> Heart sprinkles
> Brown M&M's or Reese's Pieces

1. Line a tray with parchment paper.
2. Press the cake pop mixture into the square cookie cutter, using the pressing method described in Shaping the Pops earlier in this chapter. After removing the shape from the cutter, pinch the top between your finger and thumb to make a peaked roof shape. Place shapes onto a parchment-lined tray with the pointed roofs laying sideways and chill until firm approximately 10 minutes.
3. Melt the candy coating as described in the Melting Tips section earlier in this chapter. Dip the end of each stick into the melted candy and push one stick into the flat base of each of the cake pop shapes. Return to parchment-lined tray and pop back into fridge to chill for 10 minutes.
4. Get all of the decorations ready. Sift through the cinnamon toast cereal bits to find ones that are reasonably flat, and line them up in lots of four so they will be ready when you need them.
5. Remelt the candy coating if necessary. Remove tray from fridge. Holding the end of the stick, dip a cake pop into the melted candy until the whole shape is submerged, and then lift it out of the melted candy. Holding the pop over the bowl to catch drips, gently tap the stick against your hand or the side of the bowl to remove excess candy coating.
6. Working quickly, before the candy has a chance to set, place 2 pieces of cinnamon toast cereal on each side of the "roof" to look like shingles. Top the peak of the roof with a piece of red Twizzlers.
7. On the front of the birdhouse, stick a pink heart sprinkle at the top center. Place one of the brown M&M's or Reese's Pieces underneath the heart. Place pop into the Styrofoam block.
8. Repeat for remaining pops and allow to set.

Delicate fondant butterflies alighting on each pop make this a delectable confection that will be sure to delight all. The technique for making the fondant butterflies seems a little daunting, but is actually quite easy once you have worked it out. Children as young as 5 should be able to help make them.

2 ounces Marshmallow Fondant (see Chapter 9)

Small butterfly fondant cutter (a PME small butterfly plunger cutter is ideal but not essential)

1 batch cake pop mixture (any flavor)

18 ounces pink candy coating

1. Two days prior to assembling the pops, make the butterflies. Fold a few pieces of cardboard like an accordion and line with folded parchment paper. The folds should be spaced every 2". You will need to make about 10 folds, which will give you five V-shaped valleys.

2. Dust your work surface with some cornstarch, knead the Marshmallow Fondant, and roll out to about ⅛" thickness.

3. Using the butterfly cutter, press out the butterfly shape, (if you are using a PME plunger, make sure to push down the plunger to emboss the pattern). Finally, place each butterfly shape cut-out on the folded cardboard to dry. The center of the butterfly should lay in the bottom V of a crease so that the butterfly wings dry facing upward. Repeat to make around 30 butterflies. Leave to set for 1 to 2 days.

4. When ready to make the pops, line a tray with parchment paper.

5. Shape the cake pop mixture into balls. Place onto the parchment-lined tray and chill until firm.

6. Melt the candy coating as described in the Melting Tips section earlier in this chapter. Dip the end of each stick into the melted candy and push one stick into each of the cake pop balls. Return to parchment-lined tray and pop back into the fridge to chill for 10 minutes.

7. Remelt the candy coating if necessary. Remove tray from fridge. Holding the end of the stick, dip a cake pop into the melted candy until the whole shape is submerged, and then lift it out of the melted candy. Holding the pop over the bowl to catch drips, gently tap the stick against your hand or the side of the bowl to remove excess candy coating. Remove as much excess as possible before you put the pop into the Styrofoam block.

8. Working quickly, before the candy has a chance to set, carefully press a butterfly onto the top of the pop, ensuring that the wings do not break.

9. Repeat for remaining mixture and allow to set.

Butterfly Kisses

Twinkle Star Pops

Twinkle twinkle little treat, I think you look so very sweet. These stars look great with yellow or light blue candy coating, but if you want a sparkly finish, spray on edible gold or silver luster spray, which is available at cake-decorating specialty stores. Just a quick press of the nozzle and you'll have a sky full of twinkling treats.

1 batch cake pop mixture (any flavor)

18 ounces yellow or light blue candy coating

Small (1½") star-shaped cookie or fondant cutter

1. Line a tray with parchment paper.
2. Press the cake pop mixture into the star cookie cutter, using the pressing method described in Shaping the Pops earlier in this chapter. Spend a bit of time getting the shapes flat on the top, as holes will show in the end result. Lay the shapes down flat on the parchment-lined tray.
3. Melt the candy coating as described in the Melting Tips section earlier in this chapter. Dip the end of each stick into the melted candy and then insert a stick into one of the pointed ends of each star while the shapes are still lying on the tray. Leaving the pops lying down flat, place the tray into the fridge and chill until firm.
4. Remelt the candy coating if necessary. Remove tray from fridge. Holding the end of the stick, dip a cake pop into the melted candy until the whole shape is submerged, and then lift it out of the melted candy. Holding the pop over the bowl to catch drips, gently tap the stick against your hand or the side of the bowl to remove excess candy coating. Remove as much excess as possible before you put the pop into the Styrofoam block to set.
5. Repeat for remaining pops and leave to set.

POP TIP

THESE POPS LOOK EXTRA SWEET WITH FACES DRAWN ONTO THEM. USE AN EDIBLE MARKER TO DRAW ON THE WHOLE FACE, OR STICK ON SOME EDIBLE PREMADE SUGAR EYES USING SOME OF THE EXCESS YELLOW MELTED CANDY COATING.

How much is that doggy on the lollipop stick, the one with the Tootsie Roll ears? You might be able to put a price on these Pup Pops, but watching your kids make them and sharing the memories is priceless.

> 1 batch cake pop mixture (any flavor)
> 18 ounces light brown candy coating
> Tootsie Rolls
> Red or green Froot Loops cereal
> Mini brown M&M's or premade royal icing eyes
> Black or brown jelly beans
> Edible marker

1. Line a tray with parchment paper.
2. Roll cake pop mixture into oval shapes between the palms of your hands. Place shapes onto parchment-lined tray and chill until firm.
3. Melt the candy coating as described in the Melting Tips section earlier in this chapter. Dip the end of each stick into the melted candy and push one stick into the base of each oval shape. Return to parchment-lined tray and pop back into fridge to chill for 10 minutes.
4. While the mixture is chilling, prepare the candy decorations. Make pup ears out of the Tootsie Rolls by rolling the candy out and cutting out long ear shapes, or just shape by pinching off pieces and pressing with your fingers. Gently push a lollipop stick through the center hole of each piece of Froot Loops cereal, making sure the hole is large enough to easily slip up and down the lollipop stick. Lay out the rest of the candy in groups so you can easily access them.
5. Remelt the candy coating if necessary. Remove tray from fridge. Holding the end of the stick, dip a cake pop into the melted candy until the whole shape is submerged, and then lift it out of the melted candy. Holding the pop over the bowl to catch drips, gently tap the stick against your hand or the side of the bowl to remove excess candy coating. Quickly push one of the Froot Loops up the lollipop stick from the bottom to the base of the cake pop; the melted candy should secure it to the base of the pop. Put the pop into the Styrofoam block.
6. Working quickly, before the candy sets, add the M&M's eyes or premade eyes, a jelly bean for the nose, and the Tootsie Roll ears.
7. Repeat for remaining mixture. Once the candy coating has set, use the edible marker to draw on a mouth and add a couple of dots on the cheeks.

4th of July Pops

Pack a patriotic punch with sugary star-spangled pops with Red Velvet Cake hidden inside. These look great tied with red, white, and blue striped ribbon.

1 batch Red Velvet Cake pop mixture
18 ounces white candy coating
Red and blue sprinkle mix

1. Line a tray with parchment paper.
2. Shape cake pop mixture into balls. Place onto parchment-lined tray and chill until firm.
3. Melt the candy coating as described in the Melting Tips section earlier in this chapter. Dip the end of each stick into the melted candy and push one stick into each of the cake pop balls. Return to parchment-lined tray and pop back into the fridge to chill for 10 minutes.
4. Remelt the candy coating if necessary. Remove tray from fridge. Holding the end of the stick, dip a cake pop into the melted candy until the whole shape is submerged, and then lift it out of the melted candy. Holding the pop over the bowl to catch drips, gently tap the stick against your hand or the side of the bowl to remove excess candy coating.
5. Working quickly, before the candy has a chance to set, sprinkle the red and blue sprinkles over the pop and then place it into the Styrofoam block.
6. Repeat for remaining pops and allow to set.

4th of
July Pops

AN ALTERNATIVE SERVING SUGGESTION: AFTER DIPPING, PLACE THE POPS UPSIDE DOWN ON PARCHMENT PAPER (WITH THE STICKS UPWARD), QUICKLY ADD THE SPRINKLES, AND THEN SERVE THEM IN PATRIOTIC-THEMED MINI BAKING CUPS.

◆ ◆ ◆

Batter-Up Pops

Need something to snack on while watching your favorite team? You won't strike out if you whip up these sporty treats.

1 batch cake pop mixture (any flavor)
18 ounces white candy coating
Red candy writer or edible pen

1. Line a tray with parchment paper.
2. Shape cake pop mixture into balls. Place shapes onto parchment-lined tray and chill until firm.

3. Melt the candy coating as described in the Melting Tips section earlier in this chapter. Dip the end of each stick into the melted candy and push one stick into each of the cake pop balls. Return to parchment-lined tray and pop back into the fridge to chill for 10 minutes.
4. Remelt the candy coating if necessary. Remove tray from fridge. Holding the end of the stick, dip a cake pop into the melted candy until the whole shape is submerged, and then lift it out of the melted candy. Holding the pop over the bowl to catch drips, gently tap the stick against your hand or the side of the bowl to remove excess candy coating. Remove as much excess as possible before you put the pop into the Styrofoam block to set.
5. Repeat for remaining pops. When candy coating is set, follow the directions on the candy writer to melt the chocolate and draw on stitching to represent a baseball.

POP TIP

USE RIBBONS IN YOUR FAVORITE TEAM COLORS TO DECORATE THE LOLLIPOP STICKS.

Sweet Stampin' Love Pops

Show your love for all things sweet. The stamping can be a little tricky at the start, so a few practice runs is a great idea. If you are having trouble finding stamps at your local craft shop, you can use candy conversation hearts instead. You'll need to make the sweet love stamps a day in advance.

3 ounces white Marshmallow Fondant (see Chapter 9)

Red gel food color

Small heart, lip, and cute word stamps

Nontoxic edible glitter (optional)

1 batch cake pops mixture (any flavor)

18 ounces white candy coating

1. Line a tray with parchment paper.

2. To make the sweet love stamps: Dust the work surface with some cornstarch, knead the Marshmallow Fondant, and roll it out ⅛" thick. Using a small round fondant cutter (½" to ¾"), cut out about 40 small circles. Lay them flat on the parchment paper and leave to dry for an hour or so until firm.

3. Brush a little of the red food color on the stamps and lightly press them down onto the Marshmallow Fondant rounds to stamp the designs. If you are using the nontoxic edible glitter on some of the rounds, sprinkle a little on while the food color is still wet. Allow stamped fondant rounds to dry and then brush off any excess edible glitter with a dry brush. Pick the best 24 to use on the pops and set aside.

4. When ready to make the pops line a tray with parchment paper.

5. Shape cake pop mixture into balls. Place onto parchment-lined tray and chill until firm.

6. Melt the candy coating as described in the Melting Tips section earlier in this chapter. Dip the end of each stick into the melted candy and push one stick into each of the cake pop balls. Return to parchment-lined tray and pop back into the fridge to chill for 10 minutes.

7. Remelt the candy coating if necessary. Remove tray from fridge. Holding the end of the stick, dip a cake pop into the melted candy until the whole shape is submerged, and then lift it out of the melted candy. Holding the pop over the bowl to catch drips, gently tap the stick against your hand or the side of the bowl to remove excess candy coating. Remove as much excess as possible before you put the pop into the Styrofoam block to set.

8. Working quickly, before the candy has a chance to set, press one of the round love stamps onto the pop.

9. Repeat for remaining pops and allow to set.

Sweet Stampin' Love Pops

Hot cross pops, hot cross pops, one a penny two a penny, hot cross pops. If the kids have trouble mastering the bun shape, don't let it ruin the fun; just make round pops topped with a cross. They will taste just as good.

1 batch Quick and Easy Chocolate Cake pop mixture with ½ teaspoon ground cinnamon added to the mixture

18 ounces chocolate candy coating

Royal Icing (see Chapter 9)

1. Line a tray with parchment paper.
2. Shape pop mixture into a ball and then use your fingers to mold it into a shape that is squarish at the bottom with a rounded top, similar to how a bun looks. Place shapes onto the parchment-lined tray and chill until firm.
3. Melt the candy coating as described in the Melting Tips section earlier in this chapter. Dip the end of each stick into the melted candy and push one stick into the squarish bottom side of each of the cake pops. Return to parchment-lined tray and pop back into fridge to chill for 10 minutes.
4. Remelt the candy coating if necessary. Remove tray from fridge. Holding the end of the stick, dip a cake pop into the melted candy until the whole shape is submerged, and then lift it out of the melted candy. Holding the pop over the bowl to catch drips, gently tap the stick against your hand or the side of the bowl to remove excess candy coating. Remove as much excess as possible before you put the pop into the Styrofoam block.
5. Repeat for remaining pops and allow to set.
6. Place the Royal Icing into a Ziploc bag and cut a very small hole in the corner. Practice drawing a couple of crosses on the work surface. Once you have the hang of it, draw a cross on the top of each of the "bun" cake pops.

Hot Cross Bun Pops

Leaping Laughing Frogs

Little green frog pops are as delicious as they are cute with a big laughing mouth. For a bit of fun, put some little kiss-shaped sprinkles onto the frogs' cheeks.

Mini marshmallows (or premade sugar eyes)
Black edible pen
Red Jolly Rancher candy chews
1 batch Strawberry Cake pop mixture
18 ounces light green candy coating

1. Prepare parchment paper for making frog mouths. Cut out twenty-four 1" × 1" pieces of parchment paper and fold in half to make 1" × ½" rectangles.
2. Cut each of the marshmallows in half using clean safety scissors. Using the black edible pen, draw a dot in the center of each marshmallow so they look like eyes. Cut small pieces off the Jolly Rancher candy chews and flatten into tongue shapes ¼" long.
3. Line a tray with parchment paper.
4. Shape cake pop mixture into balls. Place onto parchment-lined tray and chill until firm.
5. Melt the candy coating as described in the Melting Tips section earlier in this chapter. Dip the end of each stick into the melted candy and push one stick into each of the cake pop balls.
6. When the stick is secured, use a knife to cut a line across the front bottom of the round where you would like the mouth to be. Insert the folded parchment paper into the cut with the V of the fold pointing in toward the cake pop. You will be pulling this paper out after dipping to make an open mouth.
7. Return to parchment-lined tray and pop back into fridge to chill for 10 minutes.
8. Remelt the candy coating if necessary. Remove tray from fridge. Holding the end of the stick, dip a cake pop into the melted candy until the whole shape is submerged, and then lift it out of the melted candy. Holding the pop over the bowl to catch drips, gently tap the stick against your hand or the side of the bowl to remove excess candy coating.
9. Allow candy coating to harden a few seconds (do not allow to set) and then pull out the parchment paper to make an open mouth. If the melted candy smudges into the mouth, use the end of a spoon or lollipop stick to scrape out any candy so you can see the pink cake inside.
10. Before the mixture has a chance to set, press 2 marshmallow eyes onto the top of each cake pop and add a piece of red Jolly Rancher candy to look like a tongue. Place upright into Styrofoam block.
11. Repeat for remaining pops and allow to set completely.
12. When set, draw 2 dots on each pop for the nose just above the mouth.

These mini eggs make an "eggsellent" Easter sweet, and they can be made in any number of color combinations. Pink and brown or lilac and light green are fabulous combinations.

1 batch cake pop mixture (any flavor)

18 ounces yellow candy coating

White candy writer or royal icing in a piping bag (premade or made from Royal Icing recipe in Chapter 9)

Blue premade sugar or fondant blossoms

1. Line a tray with parchment paper.
2. Shape the cake pop mixture into egg shapes. Place the shapes onto the parchment-lined tray and chill until firm.
3. Melt the candy coating as described in the Melting Tips section earlier in this chapter. Dip the end of each stick into the melted candy and push one stick into each of the cake pop eggs. Return to parchment-lined tray and pop back into the fridge to chill for 10 minutes.
4. Remelt the candy coating if necessary. Remove tray from fridge. Holding the end of the stick, dip a cake pop into the melted candy until the whole shape is submerged, and then lift it out of the melted candy. Holding the pop over the bowl to catch drips, gently tap the stick against your hand or the side of the bowl to remove excess candy coating. Remove as much excess as possible before you put the pop into the Styrofoam block. Repeat for remaining pops and allow to set.
5. Using the candy writer or royal icing, pipe a line around the center of each pop and attach a blossom to the middle front. You can make a single line or two parallel lines or even a wavy line. To finish, pipe little dots at random around the top and bottom of each egg. Leave upright in Styrofoam block until decorations are set.

Mini lollipop look-alikes that are even sweeter than the real thing are a little challenging to make but worth it for the fun result. Little ones will have a ball working out how to measure with the string. You will need a small fondant rolling pin if you use the Marshmallow Fondant.

1 batch Quick and Easy Vanilla Cake pop mixture
18 ounces white candy coating
10 ounces pink Marshmallow Fondant (see Chapter 9)

1. Line a couple of trays with parchment paper.
2. Press the cake pop mixture into a round cookie cutter, using the pressing method described in Shaping the Pops earlier in this chapter. Spend a bit of time getting them flat on the top, as holes will show in the end result. Lay the shapes down flat on the parchment-lined tray.
3. Melt the candy coating as described in the Melting Tips section earlier in this chapter. Dip the end of each stick into the melted candy and push into the rounded side of the disk, so that the flat circle will rest on the tray. Return to parchment-lined tray and pop back into the fridge to chill for 10 minutes.
4. Remelt the candy coating if necessary. Remove tray from fridge. Holding the end of the stick, dip a cake pop into the melted candy until the whole shape is submerged, and then lift it out of the melted candy. Holding the pop over the bowl to catch drips, gently tap the stick against your hand or the side of the bowl to remove excess candy coating. Remove as much excess as possible before you put the pop into the Styrofoam block to set. Repeat for the remaining pops.
5. Using a piece of string, measure around the outside of a candy-coated pop to determine the length and width of Marshmallow Fondant you will need. Roll out some Marshmallow Fondant an inch longer than the measured length. Using a pizza cutter or other tool to get a straight line, cut the required length and width. Place the disk sideways so the curved edge of the disk is resting on the fondant and then wrap the fondant around the curved edge, pressing the fondant firmly onto the pop to secure.
6. Tidy up any excess fondant hanging over with a knife.
7. Make a long thin log of Marshmallow Fondant about ⅛" wide. Using your fingers, shape it into a swirl on the flat side of the disk. Once you are happy with the way it is sitting, press it down lightly. Use a small fondant rolling pin to press down the fondant neatly. Leave to set an hour or so.

POP TIP

IF YOU DO NOT LIKE USING MARSHMALLOW FONDANT, YOU CAN SPREAD COLORED ROYAL ICING AROUND THE EDGES OF THE CAKE POP DISK WITH A KNIFE AND PIPE A SWIRL OF ROYAL ICING ON THE FLAT SIDE OF THE LOLLI-CAKE-POP. YOU CAN BUY PREMADE ROYAL ICING MIX OR MAKE UP A BATCH OF THE RECIPE FOUND IN CHAPTER 9.

Lolli-Cake-Pops

Eyeballs on a Spike

Gruesome and ghastly treats perfect for Halloween. For an extra grisly touch, use Red Velvet Cake pop mixture if you dare.

1 batch Quick and Easy Vanilla Cake pop mixture
18 ounces white candy coating
Froot Loops cereal
Brown M&M's Minis
Red edible marker

1. Line a tray with parchment paper.
2. Shape cake pop mixture into balls. Place onto parchment-lined tray and chill until firm.
3. Melt the candy coating as described in the Melting Tips section earlier in this chapter. Dip the end of each stick into the melted candy and push one stick into each of the cake pop balls. Return to parchment-lined tray and pop back into the fridge to chill for 10 minutes.
4. Remelt the candy coating if necessary. Remove tray from fridge. Holding the end of the stick, dip a cake pop into the melted candy until the whole shape is submerged, and then lift it out of the melted candy. Holding the pop over the bowl to catch drips, gently tap the stick against your hand or the side of the bowl to remove excess candy coating. Remove as much excess as possible before you put the pop into the Styrofoam block to set. Repeat for remaining cake pops.
5. Once the pops are set, use a little of the melted candy coating to stick one M&M's Minis candy onto the top of a piece of Froot Loops cereal, and then stick the cereal onto a cake pop front and middle. Use the edible markers to draw red "veins" on the white cake pop. Repeat for remaining pops.

Eyeballs on a Spike

Scary Hairy Spider Pops

Don't save these just for Halloween—creepy crawly spider pops with their long hairy legs will be a blast to play with at any time. These pops use the easy spoon-on dipping method. The messier the finish, the better, so these are great starter pops for little ones who want to help.

1 batch cake pop mixture (any flavor)
18 ounces dark chocolate candy coating
Edible premade sugar eyes
Brown or black pipe cleaners

1. Line a cookie sheet with parchment paper.
2. Shape cake pop mixture into balls. Place onto parchment-lined tray and chill until firm.
3. Melt the candy coating as described in the Melting Tips section earlier in this chapter. Dip the end of each stick into the melted candy and push one stick into each of the cake pop balls. Return to parchment-lined tray and pop back into the fridge to chill for 10 minutes.
4. Remelt the candy coating if necessary. Remove the tray from the fridge. Hold one of the pops by the stick over the top of the bowl. Using a spoon, cover the whole pop with the candy coating. You are looking for a messy finish, so if the spooning technique does not leave the candy coating looking bumpy enough, pat it all over with the back of the spoon to make little peaks. Place in Styrofoam block. Working quickly, put 2 premade eyes near the top of the cake pop.

Scary Hairy Spider Pops

5. Repeat with remaining pops and allow to set.
6. Cut each of the pipe cleaners into 2 pieces. Wrap 4 of the cut pipe cleaners around a lollipop stick just underneath the cake pop. Bend the legs to look like spider legs. Repeat with remaining pops.

Trick or Treat Halloween Pops

The trick to making creepy nightmare-worthy cake pop treats is to find the most frightening candy decorations you can and then displaying the pops in a pail filled with monstrous decorations like super-hairy spiders or scary skeletons. Eeeeek!

1 batch cake pop mixture (any flavor)
18 ounces orange or black candy coating
Scary Halloween candy, like bats or spiders

1. Line a tray with parchment paper.
2. Shape cake pop mixture into balls. Place onto parchment-lined tray and chill until firm.
3. Melt the candy coating as described in the Melting Tips section earlier in this chapter. Dip the end of each stick into the melted candy and push one stick into each of the cake pop balls. Return to parchment-lined tray and pop back into the fridge to chill for 10 minutes.
4. Remelt the candy coating if necessary. Remove tray from fridge. Holding the end of the stick, dip a cake pop into the melted candy until the whole shape is submerged, and then lift it out of the melted candy. Holding the pop over the bowl to catch drips, gently tap the stick against your hand or the side of the bowl to remove excess candy coating. Remove as much excess as possible before you put the pop upright into the Styrofoam block. Working quickly, before the candy has a chance to set, gently push the scary candy onto each pop.
5. Repeat for remaining pops and allow to set.

Winter Wonderland Pops

Let it snow sugary treats. Pretty sugary snowflakes adorn ice-blue cake pop disks to make an elegant wintry dessert. If you're not inclined to make the snowflake decorations yourself, try sprinkling the pops with white nonpareils for a sugary-looking snowstorm effect.

4 ounces white Marshmallow Fondant (see Chapter 9)
Snowflake cutter (PME embossed plunger cutter)
1 batch cake pop mixture (any flavor)
18 ounces light blue candy coating
Round cookie cutter (2")

1. You will need to prepare the snowflakes one day before making the cake pops. Start by lining a tray with parchment paper.
2. Dust the work surface with some cornstarch, knead the Marshmallow Fondant, and roll it out ⅛" thick. Cut out about 30 snowflake shapes (2 for each pop and a couple to allow for breakages). Lay snowflakes on the parchment paper and leave to dry overnight.
3. The next day, start with lining a tray with parchment paper.
4. Press the cake pop mixture into the round 2" cookie cutter, using the pressing method described in Shaping the Pops earlier in this chapter. Spend a bit of time getting them flat on the top, as holes will show in the end result. Lay the shapes down flat on the parchment-lined tray.
5. Melt the candy coating as described in the Melting Tips section earlier in this chapter. Dip the end of each stick into the melted candy and push one stick into the round

side of each disk, so the flat circle side is still resting on the tray. Leaving the pops lying down flat, place the tray into the fridge and chill until firm.

6. Remelt the candy coating if necessary. Remove tray from fridge. Holding the end of the stick, dip a cake pop into the melted candy until the whole shape is submerged, and then lift it out of the melted candy. Holding the pop over the bowl to catch drips, gently tap the stick against your hand or the side of the bowl to remove excess candy coating. Remove as much excess as possible before you put the pop into the Styrofoam block. Working quickly, place a snowflake on each side of the pop, holding for a second until the shapes are secured to the sides.

7. Repeat for remaining pops and allow to set.

Christmas Pudding Cake Pops

Makes 12 pops

Whether you're not a fan of rich Christmas pudding or you just want to try something different, these miniature bon-bons will captivate with their Christmas cheer.

1 batch Quick and Easy Chocolate Cake pop mixture
18 ounces chocolate candy coating
½ cup Royal Icing (see Chapter 9)
Christmas sprinkles (holly leaves and berries)

1. Line a tray with parchment paper.

2. Shape cake pop mixture into balls. Place onto parchment-lined tray and chill until firm.

3. Melt the candy coating as described in the Melting Tips section earlier in this chapter. Dip the end of each stick into the melted candy and push one stick into each of the cake pop balls. Return to parchment-lined tray and pop back into the fridge to chill for 10 minutes.

4. Remelt the candy coating if necessary. Remove tray from fridge. Holding the end of the stick, dip a cake pop into the melted candy until the whole shape is submerged, and then lift it out of the melted candy. Holding the pop over the bowl to catch drips, gently tap the stick against your hand or the side of the bowl to remove excess candy coating. Remove as much excess as possible before you put the pop into the Styrofoam block to set. Repeat for remaining pops.

5. Once the pops are set, put the Royal Icing into a Ziploc bag and pipe a wavy, uneven shape of icing onto the top of each pop to look like Christmas pudding icing. Before the Royal Icing sets, carefully place the holly and sprinkles onto the top of each pop.

CHAPTER 3

Cupcake Pops

Everyone loves mini cupcakes and muffins, and when you pop them onto a wooden skewer they become even more captivating. Store decorated cupcakes in airtight containers for up to two days if required and then pop them onto skewers just before serving. Make sure you tie a short length of ribbon just under each cupcake. This not only makes it look cute, but it also stops your delicious treat from sliding down the skewer. Muffins are best skewered and eaten the same day. The next two recipes can be used for every cupcake pop in the rest of the chapter, but feel free to get creative and use other cupcake recipes!

Quick and Easy Mini Vanilla Cupcakes

Makes 24 mini cupcakes

This light and delicious mini cupcake is made in a few easy steps, and there's next to no clean-up time with only one bowl to wash up afterward. This recipe takes the cake for sure.

¾ cup self-rising flour

⅔ cup sugar

1 stick plus 2 tablespoons (5 ounces) unsalted butter at room temperature

3 eggs

½ teaspoon vanilla extract

1. Preheat oven to 350°F. Place 24 mini baking cups into nonstick mini-cupcake pans.
2. Sift the flour and sugar into a large bowl, make a well in the center, and then add in the remaining ingredients. Mix well at low using a hand mixer until just combined.
3. Scrape down the sides of the bowl and then mix at medium-high speed for 2 minutes.
4. Spoon heaped tablespoons of the mixture into nonstick mini-cupcake pans.
5. Bake for 10–12 minutes until a toothpick inserted in the center comes out clean. Remove from oven and allow to cool for 5 minutes before turning out on a wire rack to cool.

Quick and Easy Mini Chocolate Cupcakes

Makes 24 mini cupcakes

One-bowl pour-and-mix cupcakes are a breeze to bake. Team them with a simple chocolate glaze and they'll be a dream to decorate and eat as well.

⅔ cup all-purpose flour

¼ cup unsweetened cocoa powder

½ cup sugar

1½ teaspoons baking powder

½ teaspoon vanilla extract

¼ cup vegetable oil

2 eggs at room temperature

½ cup whole milk

1. Preheat oven to 325°F. Place 24 mini baking cups into nonstick mini-cupcake pans.
2. Sift all the dry ingredients into a large bowl, make a well in the center, and then add in the remaining ingredients. Mix well at low using a hand mixer until just combined.
3. Scrape down the sides of the bowl and then mix at medium-high speed for 2 minutes.
4. Spoon heaped tablespoons of mixture into nonstick mini-cupcake pans.
5. Bake for 14–16 minutes until a toothpick inserted in the center comes out clean. Remove from oven and allow to cool for 5 minutes before turning out on a wire rack to cool.

Mini Cupcake Kabobs

You can't go wrong with these impressive cupcake kabobs. You can use any type of cupcake combination and frosting that you like. Arranging the cupcakes and candy on the kabobs is an ideal task for little kids to teach them about patterns.

> 1 batch Quick and Easy Mini Vanilla Cupcakes (baked and cooled)
>
> 1 batch Quick and Easy Mini Chocolate Cupcakes (baked and cooled)
>
> 1 batch Vanilla Buttercream Frosting (see Chapter 2)
> Gumdrops

1. Spread vanilla frosting on the top of each cupcake.
2. Holding the sides of a vanilla cupcake, gently press the cupcake down onto the skewer, stopping when the bottom of the cupcake is about 4" from the top.
3. Push a gumdrop onto the skewer on top of the cupcake, and then gently push a chocolate cupcake onto the skewer.
4. Finish off with a gumdrop candy. It should just fit onto the top of the skewer without any of the wooden end poking out. Move the rest of the cupcakes and candy up or down as required.
5. Using the first kabob as a guide, assemble the remaining skewers with the rest of the ingredients. Tie some ribbon on each skewer under the bottom cupcake to help keep it in place when upright.

Mini Flower Cupcakes

Delicious candy bits are arranged on the mini cupcakes to create a pleasing posy of flowers. These cupcakes are a great place to start for beginner decorators.

> 1 batch Quick and Easy Mini Vanilla Cupcakes (baked and cooled)
>
> ½ batch Vanilla Buttercream Frosting (see Chapter 2)
> Yellow M&M's or Skittles
> 1 packet pink and white mini marshmallows

1. Spread the vanilla frosting evenly over the top of each cupcake.
2. Place a yellow candy in the center of each cupcake, pressing down lightly to secure it to the frosting.
3. Using safety scissors, snip the marshmallows in half. Press marshmallow halves in a circle around the yellow candy to look like petals.
4. Insert skewers into Styrofoam blocks. Near the top of each skewer, about ¾" from the top, tie on a small length of green ribbon with a knot. The ribbon will keep the cupcake from sliding down the skewer.
5. Holding the sides of the cupcake, gently press the cupcake down onto the skewer until it seems secure and the ribbon is holding it in place.

PBJ and Chocolate Bites

Peanut Butter Frosting looks so pretty when piped with a big swirl on the cupcakes. However, if you don't have a piping set, you can just pile on the frosting with the flat side of a knife. Put on as much as you can; in this case, the more frosting, the better.

1 batch Quick and Easy Mini Chocolate Cupcakes (baked and cooled)

¾ cup strawberry jelly

Peanut Butter Frosting (see Chapter 9)

Reese's Pieces

1. Using a spoon, scoop a small hole about ½ teaspoon in size in the top of each cupcake. Fill each hole with ½ teaspoon of strawberry jelly.
2. Fit a large star tip to a piping bag and fill the bag with Peanut Butter Frosting.
3. Use even and gentle pressure to swirl a generous amount of frosting onto the top of each cupcake. Top each with one or more Reese's Pieces.
4. Insert skewers into Styrofoam blocks. Near the top of each skewer, about ¾" from the top, tie on a small length of ribbon with a knot. The ribbon will keep the cupcake from sliding down the skewer.
5. Holding the sides of the cupcake, gently press the cupcake down onto the skewer until it seems secure and the ribbon is holding it in place.

POP TIP

TRY TOPPING THESE DELICIOUS BITS WITH CHOPPED PEANUT BUTTER CUPS INSTEAD OF REESE'S PIECES!

PBJ and Chocolate Bites

Sunny
Oreo Cookie
Bouquet

Sunny Oreo Cookie Bouquet

A beautiful bunch of flower cupcakes with a cookie center that can brighten up any day. Get the kids to practice piping on a clean piece of parchment paper before starting on the cupcakes.

Piping bag fitted with #68 tip

1 batch Vanilla Buttercream Frosting (see Chapter 2) or Cream Cheese Frosting (see Chapter 9) colored yellow

1 batch Quick and Easy Mini Chocolate Cupcakes (baked and cooled)

Mini Oreo cookies

1. Fit the #68 tip to the piping bag and fill with the yellow buttercream frosting. Pipe a small dot of buttercream in the center of the mini cupcake.
2. Working around the edge of the cupcake, pipe sunflower petals by placing the edge of the piping tip against the cupcake, applying slight pressure to the piping bag for a second while pulling away from the cupcake, and then releasing the pressure while continuing to pull the tip away. Pipe all the way around the cupcake at least 2 times.
3. Place a mini Oreo cookie in the center of the cupcake, pressing down lightly with your fingertip to secure.
4. Insert skewers into Styrofoam blocks. Near the top of each skewer, about ¾" from the top, tie on a small length of ribbon with a knot. The ribbon will keep the cupcake from sliding down the skewer.
5. Holding the sides of the cupcake, gently press the cupcake down onto the skewer until it seems secure and the ribbon is holding it in place.

POP TIP

IF YOU DON'T HAVE A PIPING TIP, JUST PIPE ROUND DOLLOPS OF BUTTERCREAM.

◆◆◆

Malty Mini Chocolate Cakes

Chocolate cupcakes frosted with malt-infused chocolate and topped with a malted milk ball makes this a recipe for yumminess.

2 tablespoons Original Ovaltine

1 batch Chocolate Buttercream Frosting (see Chapter 2)

1 batch Quick and Easy Mini Chocolate Cupcakes (baked and cooled)

Whoppers

1. Beat the Ovaltine into the chocolate frosting until well combined.
2. Top each cupcake with a swirl of the frosting and then place one Whopper on top of each swirl.
3. Insert skewers into Styrofoam blocks. Near the top of each skewer, about ¾" from the top, tie on small length of ribbon with a knot. The ribbon will keep the cupcake from sliding down the skewer.
4. Holding the sides of the cupcake, gently press the cupcake down onto the skewer until it seems secure and the ribbon is holding it in place.

Perfectly pink cupcakes will add a touch of girly glamour to any party, play date, or afternoon tea. Let the kids go crazy and add as many pink-licious decorations as the cupcake can hold.

> 1 batch Quick and Easy Mini Vanilla Cupcakes baked in pink mini baking cups (cooled)
>
> 1 batch Vanilla Buttercream Frosting (see Chapter 2) or Raspberry Buttercream (see Chapter 9) colored bright pink
>
> 8 mini pink Tootsie Fruit Rolls
>
> Pink sugar and sprinkles
>
> Optional: mini pink sugar flowers, pink M&M's, and silver sprinkles

1. Cut each of the mini Tootsie Rolls into 3 pieces and roll into rounds; you will end up with 24.
2. Pop a large piping tip, like Wilton 1M or 195, into the end of a piping bag. Fill the bag about ⅔ full with the pink frosting. Twist the end of the piping bag closed. Using steady pressure, pipe a swirl on the top of each cupcake. If you don't have a piping bag, use a flat knife and pile the pink frosting high on top of the cupcake.
3. Place one of the Tootsie Roll rounds on the top of each cupcake.
4. Place each of the pink decorations in a separate bowl on a table. Place each cupcake on a large plate (to catch extra sprinkles) and let the kids add their own decorations.
5. Insert skewers into Styrofoam blocks. Near the top of each skewer, about ¾" from the top, tie on a small length of pink ribbon with a knot. The ribbon will keep the cupcake from sliding down the skewer.
6. Holding the sides of the cupcake, gently press the cupcake down onto the skewer until it seems secure and the ribbon is holding it in place.

Pretty in Pink Cupcakes

Everyone will be asking for some more of these cupcakes! If you'd like to make them a little bit more authentic, you could quickly grill the marshmallows in the oven, but be quick and careful as they will be hot.

1 cup self-rising flour

1 teaspoon cinnamon

⅔ cup untoasted wheat germ

1 stick plus 2 tablespoons (5 ounces) unsalted butter

1 cup packed light brown sugar

3 tablespoons honey

2 large eggs

1 teaspoon vanilla extract

½ cup whipping cream

2 tablespoons unsalted butter

1¼ cups (8 ounces) semisweet chocolate chips (or chopped chocolate)

Large marshmallows

1. To make the cupcakes, preheat oven to 325°F. Line two 12-compartment mini-muffin pans with mini baking cups.
2. Sift together the flour and cinnamon. Mix in the wheat germ and set aside.
3. In a large bowl on medium-high speed, mix together the 1¼ sticks butter, sugar, and honey until light and fluffy, about 3 minutes. Reduce speed to medium low and mix in the eggs one at a time, scraping down the sides of the bowl between each addition. Mix in the vanilla extract.
4. Reduce speed to low and add the flour mixture, mixing until combined.
5. Spoon the mixture into the prepared pans. Bake for 15 minutes until golden and a toothpick inserted in the center comes out clean. Remove from oven and allow to cool for 5 minutes before turning out on a wire rack to cool.
6. Place the cream and 2 tablespoons butter in a large microwave-safe bowl and heat at high for 40 seconds. Remove from microwave and stir in the chocolate chips. Mix until all the chocolate is melted. If some chocolate does not completely melt, return mixture to microwave and heat at medium low for 60 seconds. Remove from microwave and stir again. Leave at room temperature to thicken for 1–2 hours.
7. Insert skewers into Styrofoam blocks. Near the top of each skewer, about ¾" from the top, tie on a small length of ribbon with a knot. The ribbon will keep the cupcake from sliding down the skewer.
8. To assemble, dollop a heaped teaspoon of the chocolate mixture on the top of each cupcake and swirl it around with the back of the spoon.
9. Cut the marshmallows in half using clean safety scissors, and press one half on the top of each chocolate-topped cupcake.
10. Holding the sides of the cupcake, gently push down the cupcake onto the skewer.

Bitty Banana Cakes with Cream Cheese Frosting

Makes 24

These moist little bites of banana cake will be delicious with or without the cream cheese frosting. If your kids are already sweet enough, you can omit the frosting step and just sprinkle with a little powdered sugar.

> **3 bananas**
> **1 egg**
> **1½ cups self-rising flour**
> **½ cup sugar**
> **¼ teaspoon salt**
> **⅓ cup oil**
> **1 teaspoon vanilla**
> **1 batch Cream Cheese Frosting (see Chapter 9)**

1. Preheat oven to 325°F. Line two 12-compartment mini-muffin pans with mini baking cups. Have the kids mash the bananas well in a large bowl.
2. Add the remaining ingredients, except the frosting to the bowl and stir with a large spoon until the mixture is just blended. Divide the batter evenly among the muffin cups.
3. Pop both the pans in the preheated oven and bake for 20 minutes or until golden and a toothpick inserted comes out clean.
4. Place the frosting into a piping bag with a star tip and pipe a swirl onto the top of each mini cake. If you do not have a piping bag, just spoon a dollop onto each cake.
5. Insert skewers into Styrofoam blocks. Near the top of each skewer, about ¾" from the top, tie on a small length of ribbon with a knot. The ribbon will keep the cupcake from sliding down the skewer.
6. Holding the sides of the cupcake, gently press the cupcake down onto the skewer until it seems secure and the ribbon is holding it in place.

POP TIP

TRY ADDING ½ CUP DRIED FRUIT OR MINI CHOCOLATE CHIPS WHEN ADDING THE OTHER INGREDIENTS TO JAZZ UP THESE CAKES.

Double Chocolate Chip and Spice Mini Muffins

Makes 24

A sneaky serving of whole wheat flour adds extra fiber and wholesome goodness to these otherwise decadent lightly spiced cakelets.

2 cups whole wheat self-rising flour

¼ cup cocoa powder

½ teaspoon baking soda

2 teaspoons ground cinnamon

¾ cup chocolate chips

½ cup vegetable oil

¾ cup buttermilk

2 large eggs

¾ cup superfine sugar

1. Preheat over to 375°F. Grease two 12-compartment mini-muffin pans.
2. Sift flour, cocoa, baking soda, and cinnamon into a large bowl to remove lumps. Tip any of the whole wheat flour husks that remain in the sifter into bowl with the already sifted flour. Add the chocolate chips.
3. In a separate bowl, whisk together the oil, buttermilk, eggs, and sugar until combined. Add to dry ingredients and stir until just combined.
4. Spoon the mixture into the mini-muffin pan cups until it is heaped just over the rim.
5. Bake for 14–16 minutes until the muffins are golden and a toothpick inserted into the center comes out clean. Leave to cool in pans for a minute before turning out onto wire rack to cool.
6. Insert skewers into Styrofoam blocks. Near the top of each skewer, about ¾" from the top, tie on a small length of ribbon with a knot. The ribbon will keep the muffin from sliding down the skewer.
7. Holding the sides of the cupcake, gently press the muffin down onto the skewer until it seems secure and the ribbon is holding it in place.

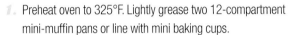

Blueberry and White Chocolate Mini Muffins

Makes 24

Succulent blueberries merge with white chocolate chips to create morsels that would make a dramatic addition to any breakfast or brunch buffet.

2 cups self-rising flour

½ cup firmly packed brown sugar

½ cup white chocolate chips

¾ cup buttermilk

½ cup vegetable oil

1 egg

1 cup blueberries, fresh or frozen

1. Preheat oven to 325°F. Lightly grease two 12-compartment mini-muffin pans or line with mini baking cups.
2. Sift the flour and sugar into a large bowl. Mix in the white chocolate chips.
3. Add the buttermilk, oil, and egg and mix with a large spoon until the mixture is just combined. Gently fold in the blueberries.
4. Spoon the mixture into the mini-muffin pan cups until it is heaped just over the rim.
5. Bake for 15–17 minutes until the muffins are golden and a toothpick inserted in the center comes out clean. Leave to cool in pans for a minute before turning out onto wire rack to cool.
6. Insert skewers into Styrofoam blocks. Near the top of each skewer, about ¾" from the top, tie on a small length of ribbon with a knot. The ribbon will keep the muffin from sliding down the skewer.
7. Holding the sides of the cupcake, gently press the muffin down onto the skewer until it seems secure and the ribbon is holding it in place.

Blueberry and White Chocolate Mini Muffins

CHAPTER 4

Cookie Pops

Why take a perfectly acceptable cookie and pop it on a stick? Why, to make it even more fun to eat, of course! Each of these recipes has been tested to make sure it will hold up to perfect upstanding pop standards. There are two main types of cookies included in this chapter; bake-and-eat cookies, and decorated sugar cookies. First, we'll start with the cookies you can just make and put on a stick.

Full of Chocolate Chips Cookies

Makes 18

Crisp cookies that won't fall off the stick and are filled with stacks of chocolate chips make this a hard-to-beat favorite treat on a stick.

- 1½ cups all-purpose flour
- ¼ teaspoon baking soda
- ½ teaspoon salt
- 1 stick (4 ounces) unsalted butter at room temperature
- ¼ cup granulated sugar
- ½ cup packed light brown sugar
- 1 teaspoon vanilla extract
- 1 large egg at room temperature
- 1 cup milk chocolate chips (about 6 ounces)

1. Preheat oven to 350°F. Line 2 or 3 baking cookie sheets (depending on their size) with parchment paper.
2. Sift together the flour, baking soda, and salt. Set aside.
3. In the bowl of an electric mixer at medium-high speed combine the butter and both sugars until light and fluffy. Reduce speed to low and add the vanilla and egg. Scrape down the edges of the bowl with a spatula.
4. With the mixer still on low, add the flour mixture. Once combined, add the chocolate chips, scraping the sides of the bowl as required.
5. Drop 1½-tablespoon amounts of dough onto the parchment-lined cookie sheets, leaving enough room to spread. Insert a lollipop stick approximately 1" into the side of each cookie so the stick is lying flat parallel to the cookie sheet.
6. Bake for 8–10 minutes or until cookie starts to turn golden around edges
7. Allow the cookies to cool on the trays for 5 minutes, and then using a spatula carefully remove to a wire rack to cool.

POP TIP

USE SEMISWEET CHOCOLATE OR PEANUT BUTTER CHIPS OR A MIXTURE TO MAKE THESE COOKIES THE PERFECT TASTE MATCH FOR YOUR FAMILY.

Happy Dot Cookies

Makes 20 large cookies

You'll have a hard time working out what makes the kids happier with these cookies, pushing the M&M's into the tops of the unbaked cookies or eating them. Either way it's happy smiles and giggles all around.

1¼ cup self-rising flour

3 tablespoons cocoa

1 stick (4 ounces) unsalted butter, room temperature

½ cup sugar

½ cup brown sugar

1 egg

½ cup semisweet chocolate chips

½ cup M&M's

1. Preheat oven to 325°F. Line 2 or 3 cookie sheets (depending on their size) with parchment paper.
2. Sift together the flour and cocoa. Set aside.
3. In a large bowl beat butter and sugars at high speed until creamy. Reduce speed to medium low and beat in egg.
4. At a low speed, mix in flour and cocoa mixture. Fold in the semisweet chocolate chips.
5. Roll into tablespoon-size balls and place on the cookie sheet. Press down lightly with fingertips or fork and insert the lollipop stick into the side of each cookie so the stick is lying flat parallel to the cookie sheet. Decorate the cookie with the M&M's.
6. Bake for 15 minutes. Allow the cookies to cool on the trays for 5 minutes, and then using a spatula carefully remove to a wire rack to cool.

Packed with Peanuts Cookies

Makes 24 cookies

Only four ingredients and one bowl make these cookies as much of a treat to make as to eat, and as an extra bonus, they are gluten free. These cookies are just as delicious if you use chocolate chips in place of the peanuts.

1½ cups peanut butter

1 cup sugar

1 egg lightly beaten

1 cup peanuts

1. Preheat oven to 350°F. Line 2 or 3 cookie sheets (depending on their size) with parchment paper.
2. In a large mixing bowl stir the peanut butter, sugar, and egg with a wooden spoon until combined. Add the peanuts and mix well.
3. Place 1½ tablespoons of the mixture on the prepared cookie sheets and flatten slightly. Push a lollipop stick into the side of each mound of cookie dough so the stick is lying flat parallel to the cookie sheet.
4. Bake for 14–18 minutes until the cookies are darker all over and golden around the edges. Allow the cookies to cool on the trays completely before using a spatula to carefully remove them. These cookies will crumble easily until they are cooled.

Oatmeal Raisin Spice Cookies

Makes 18

These easy-to-make, easy-to-eat wholesome cookies will fast become a household favorite. Add ¼ cup of chopped walnuts when combining the oats and raisins for a nutty, hearty-tasting cookie.

1½ cups all-purpose flour

¼ teaspoon baking soda

1 teaspoon cinnamon

½ teaspoon salt

1 stick (4 ounces) unsalted butter at room temperature

¼ cup granulated sugar

½ cup packed light brown sugar

1 teaspoon vanilla extract

1 large egg at room temperature

¾ cup rolled oats

¾ cup raisins

1. Preheat oven to 350°F. Line 2 or 3 cookie sheets (depending on their size) with parchment paper.

2. Sift together the flour, baking soda, cinnamon, and salt. Set aside.

3. In the bowl of an electric mixer at medium-high speed combine the butter and both sugars until light and fluffy. Reduce speed to low and add the vanilla and egg. Scrape down the edges of the bowl with a spatula.

4. With the mixer still on low, add the flour mixture. Once combined, add the oats and raisins, scraping the sides of the bowl as required.

5. Drop 1½-tablespoon amounts of dough onto the parchment-lined cookie sheets, leaving enough room for cookies to spread. Insert a lollipop stick about 1" into the side of each cookie so the stick is lying flat parallel to the cookie sheet.

6. Bake for 8–10 minutes or until cookie starts to turn golden around edges. Allow the cookies to cool on the trays for 5 minutes, and then using a spatula, carefully remove to a wire rack to cool.

Dark and Dangerous Triple Chocolate Cookies

Makes 25

Warning! These cookies are so good you won't want to stop eating them. Plus they are extra easy to make—just melt and mix, with no electric mixer needed. Let each of the kids have a turn mixing with a big wooden spoon and share the fun.

1½ cups all-purpose flour
¾ cup cocoa powder
1½ cups soft brown sugar
1½ sticks (6 ounces) unsalted butter
⅔ cup heaped (5 ounces) semisweet chocolate, chopped
2 large eggs, lightly beaten
¾ cup dark chocolate chips
¾ cup white chocolate chips

1. Preheat oven to 375°F. Line 2 or 3 cookie sheets (depending on their size) with parchment paper.
2. Sift flour, cocoa, and brown sugar into a mixing bowl. Set aside.
3. Combine butter and chopped semisweet chocolate in a bowl and melt in microwave in short bursts at medium low, mixing well between each session. Add chocolate mixture and eggs to dry ingredients and mix until combined. Do not overbeat. Stir in all chocolate chips.
4. Drop 1½-tablespoon amounts of dough onto cookie sheet and flatten slightly. Push a lollipop stick into the side of each cookie so the stick is lying flat parallel to the cookie sheet.
5. Bake for 12 minutes. Allow the cookies to cool on the trays for 5 minutes, and then using a spatula, carefully remove to a wire rack to cool.

POP TIP

REPLACE ½ CUP OF THE CHOCOLATE CHIPS WITH MACADAMIA NUT HALVES, OR FOR DEEPLY DARK CHOCOLATE COOKIES REPLACE ALL THE WHITE CHOCOLATE CHIPS WITH DARK.

Makes about 36

Tricky to say, yummy to eat, snickerdoodle cookie pops are a super-scrumptious treat! The combination of butter, cinnamon, and vanilla makes for an outstanding cookie. Rolling the cookies in the sugar is a great place for beginner bakers to help out.

> 2¾ cups all-purpose flour
>
> 2 teaspoons cream of tartar
>
> 1 teaspoon baking soda
>
> ½ teaspoon salt
>
> ½ cup sugar
>
> 2 teaspoons cinnamon
>
> 1 stick (4 ounces) unsalted butter at room temperature
>
> ½ cup (8 tablespoons) Crisco or other vegetable shortening
>
> 1½ cups sugar
>
> 1 teaspoon vanilla extract
>
> 2 large eggs

1. Preheat oven to 350°F. Line 2 or 3 cookie sheets (depending on their size) with parchment paper.
2. Sift together the flour, cream of tartar, baking soda, and salt into a bowl. In a separate bowl mix together ½ cup sugar and the cinnamon. Set aside until needed.
3. In the bowl of an electric mixer on medium speed beat the butter, vegetable shortening, and 1½ cups sugar until smooth and fluffy, around 3 minutes. Add the vanilla and the eggs one at a time, stopping the mixer and scraping down the sides of the bowl as required. Reduce speed to low and add the flour mixture, mixing until just combined.
4. Take 1½ tablespoons of the dough and roll into a ball between the palms of your hands. Pop into the cinnamon-sugar mixture and coat the cookie dough well. Place onto a parchment-lined cookie sheet, leaving space for lollipop sticks and spreading.
5. Gently flatten the top of each cookie and then insert a lollipop stick at least 1" into the side of each cookie so the stick is lying flat parallel to the cookie sheet.
6. Bake for 10–12 minutes or until golden. Allow the cookies to cool on the trays for 5 minutes, and then using a spatula, carefully remove to a wire rack to cool.

Scrumptious Snickerdoodle Pops

Jolly Green Giant Thumbprint Cookies

Makes about 36

These cookies look gruesome, but they taste of buttery home-baked goodness. Red jelly or jam looks particularly good against the green cookie dough.

3 cups all-purpose flour

¼ teaspoon salt

2 sticks (8 ounces) unsalted butter at room temperature

½ cup firmly packed brown sugar

1 large egg

1 teaspoon vanilla extract

Few drops green gel food color

½ cup red jelly (like strawberry or raspberry)

1. Preheat oven to 350°F. Line 2 or 3 cookie sheets (depending on their size) with parchment paper.
2. Sift together the flour and salt. Set aside.
3. In a large bowl beat butter and sugar at high speed until creamy. Reduce speed to medium low and beat in egg, vanilla, and green food color.
4. Reduce the speed to low and mix in the flour and salt mixture.
5. Roll 1 tablespoon of dough into a ball. Place each ball onto a prepared cookie sheets and press an indent into the middle with your thumb. Cute little kiddy-sized thumbs may need to wiggle around a little bit to make a giant-sized indent. Fill the indent with ½ teaspoon of jelly. Gently push the lollipop sticks into the side of the cookie dough so the stick is lying flat parallel to the cookie sheet.
6. Bake 10–12 minutes until lightly browned. Allow the cookies to cool on the trays for 5 minutes, and then using a spatula, carefully remove to a wire rack to cool.

Fudgy Chocolate Chip Sandwich Cookies

Makes around 20 sandwiches

Buy ready-made cookies from the supermarket or make your own by following the Full of Chocolate Chips Cookies recipe in this chapter. Either way, you'll be heading back for more of these fudgy delights.

½ cup cream

2 tablespoons (1 ounce) unsalted butter

1⅓ cups (8 ounces) semisweet chocolate chips (or chopped chocolate)

14-ounce package chocolate chip cookies (around 40 cookies)

1. Place the cream and butter in a large microwave-safe bowl and heat at high for 40 seconds. Remove from microwave and stir in the chocolate chips. Mix until all the chocolate is melted. If some chocolate does not completely melt, return to microwave and heat at medium low for 60 seconds, remove from microwave, and stir again.
2. Leave at room temperature to thicken for around 1–2 hours, or pop in fridge to speed up chilling.
3. Line a cookie sheet with parchment paper and place half the cookies on the sheet. Top with 1 teaspoon of chocolate mixture. Place a lollipop stick on top of the cookie and the chocolate mixture and then top with another cookie, pressing down gently. Leave to set at room temperature for another hour.

Nutella Pinwheels

Makes 30

These refrigerator cookies look unassuming until you cut through to see the swirly middle. Give the kids a safe knife and let them slice away.

- 1½ cups all purpose flour
- ¼ teaspoon salt
- 2 sticks (8 ounces) unsalted butter at room temperature
- ⅔ cup superfine sugar
- 1 egg yolk
- ½ teaspoon vanilla extract
- ½ cup Nutella (chocolate hazelnut spread)

1. Sift together flour and salt. Set aside.
2. Mix butter and sugar in a large bowl with a wooden spoon. Beat in the egg yolk and vanilla and then add the flour and salt mixture. Stir until combined. Wrap the dough in plastic wrap and pop in the fridge for an hour.
3. Remove dough from fridge, unwrap, and roll out between 2 sheets of parchment paper into a 12" square. Spread the Nutella evenly over the dough and then roll up like a jellyroll to form a log. Wrap in plastic wrap and chill in fridge again for 30 minutes.
4. Preheat the oven to 375°F. Line 2 or 3 cookie sheets (depending on their size) with parchment paper.
5. Unwrap the roll and cut into thin slices with a knife. Lay the slices on the cookie sheets with room to spread and insert a lollipop stick into the side of each round so the stick is lying flat parallel to the cookie sheet.
6. Bake in the oven for 10–15 minutes until golden brown. Allow to cool on cookie sheets for 5 minutes and then transfer carefully to wire racks to cool completely.

Zingy Citrus Sugar Cookies

Makes about 3 dozen

Tongue-tingling, fresh-tasting citrus cookies are just the thing for a jaded palate.

- 2¾ cups all-purpose flour
- 1 teaspoon baking soda
- ½ teaspoon baking powder
- ¼ teaspoon salt
- 1 stick (8 ounces) unsalted butter at room temperature
- 1½ cups sugar
- 1 large egg
- Zest of 2 large lemons
- 2 tablespoons lemon juice
- 1 teaspoon vanilla extract
- ½ cup sugar

1. Preheat oven to 350°F. Line 2 or 3 cookie sheets (depending on their size) with parchment paper.
2. Sift the flour, baking soda, baking powder, and salt together; set aside.
3. In a large bowl, using an electric mixer, beat the butter and 1½ cups sugar at high speed until light and fluffy. Add the egg, zest, lemon juice, and vanilla. Mix at medium low until just combined.
4. Put ½ cup sugar in a shallow bowl. Shape 1 tablespoon of dough into a ball and roll in sugar. Pop onto the cookie sheets, leaving enough space to spread. Insert a lollipop stick about ½" into the side of each cookie, so the stick is lying flat parallel to the cookie sheet.
5. Bake for 10–12 minutes until golden on edges. Allow the cookies to cool on the trays for 5 minutes, and then using a spatula, carefully remove to a wire rack to cool.

Chunky Cherry, Coconut, and White Chocolate Cookies

Makes 18

These flavors combine to make a super taste explosion! Dark chocolate chips can be substituted for the white to give the cookies a deeper, more intense flavor burst.

1½ cups all-purpose flour

¼ teaspoon baking soda

1 teaspoon cinnamon

½ teaspoon salt

1 stick (4 ounces) unsalted butter at room temperature

¼ cup granulated sugar

½ cup packed light brown sugar

1 teaspoon vanilla extract

1 large egg at room temperature

1½ cups shredded coconut

1 cup dried cherries

1 cup white chocolate chips

1. Preheat oven to 350°F. Line 2 or 3 cookie sheets (depending on their size) with parchment paper.
2. Sift together the flour, baking soda, cinnamon, and salt. Set aside.
3. In the bowl of an electric mixer at medium-high speed combine the butter and both sugars until light and fluffy. Reduce speed to low and add the vanilla and egg. Scrape down the edges of the bowl with a spatula.
4. With the mixer still on low add the flour mixture. Once combined, mix in the coconut, dried cherries, and white chocolate chips, scraping down the sides of the bowl as required.
5. Drop 1½-tablespoon amounts of dough onto the parchment-lined cookie sheets, leaving enough room for the cookies to spread. Insert a lollipop stick about 1" into the side of each cookie so the stick is lying flat parallel to the cookie sheet.
6. Bake for 8–10 minutes or until cookie starts to turn golden around edges. Allow the cookies to cool on the trays for 5 minutes, and then using a spatula, carefully remove to a wire rack to cool.

PLAY-DOUGH COOKIE RECIPES

This cookie dough is perfect for little kids to work with. No need to roll it out flat, just shape as you would Play-Doh. The best part, of course, is that you can bake and eat these little works of art.

◆ ◆ ◆

Play-Dough Cookies

Make 24 regular or 12 jumbo cookies

Mix up a batch of this dough and watch the kids create an edible masterpiece. The dough can be colored by kneading drops of gel food colors into the dough until you achieve the color you're looking for.

- 2¾ cups all-purpose flour
- 1 teaspoon baking powder
- ¼ teaspoon salt
- 1½ sticks (6 ounces) unsalted butter at room temperature
- 3 ounces cream cheese
- 1 cup sugar
- 1 egg
- 1 teaspoon vanilla extract
- Gel food colors

1. Preheat oven to 350°F. Line 2 or 3 cookie sheets (depending on their size) with parchment paper.
2. Sift together the flour, baking powder, and salt. Set aside.
3. In a large bowl, using an electric mixer, cream the butter, cream cheese, and sugar at high speed until light and fluffy. Reduce speed to medium low, add the egg and vanilla, and mix until combined. Scrape down the sides of the bowl as required.
4. Reduce speed to low and mix in the flour mixture until just combined.
5. Add food color as desired, and use like Play-Doh to make shaped cookies.
6. Bake until the cookie turns golden around the edges and the centers are set. A 2½" cookie will take approximately 8–10 minutes to bake.

Over the Rainbow Cookies

Make 12 cookies

These cookies are just so much fun to create. Make them in traditional rainbow colors as suggested in the recipe or change the colors to pastel or even different shades of the same color.

1 batch Play-Dough Cookies dough
Red, blue, green, yellow, and purple gel food colors

1. Line 2 or 3 cookie sheets (depending on their size) with parchment paper.
2. Divide the dough into 10 equal pieces and color each section by kneading the gel food color in as follows:

   4 pieces purple
   2 pieces blue
   2 pieces green
   1 piece yellow
   1 piece red

3. Break off sections of the dough for each cookie and roll into thin logs. A good guide is to use about 1½ tablespoons purple, 1 tablespoon blue, 1 tablespoon green, ½ tablespoon yellow, and ½ tablespoon red for each cookie.

4. Place the colored logs next to each other on the parchment paper, forming a rainbow. Flatten them together slightly with your fingertips. Repeat until all the dough is used, and then insert a lollipop stick into each cookie.
5. Place cookie sheets in fridge to chill for 10 minutes. Preheat oven to 350°F.
6. Bake cookies for about 16 minutes until the mixture just starts to turn golden around the edges and is set in the middle. Remove from oven and cool on the cookie sheets for 5–10 minutes or until you can safely remove them with a spatula without disturbing the lollipop sticks.

IF YOU LIKE, YOU CAN USE A LITTLE ROYAL ICING (SEE CHAPTER 9) TO STICK SOME MARSHMALLOWS ON THE ENDS OF EACH SIDE OF THE RAINBOW TO LOOK LIKE CLOUDS.

Mustache Cookies

This funny and quirky idea for a cookie will have everyone giggling in delight as they use this treat as a dress-up disguise.

¼ cup unsweetened cocoa powder
Black or dark brown gel food color
½ batch Play-Dough Cookies dough

1. Line 2 or 3 cookie sheets (depending on their size) with parchment paper.
2. Mix the cocoa and enough black or dark brown food color into the cookie dough to achieve the desired color.
3. Break off 4 tablespoons of dough and shape into a log around 3" long. Flatten the log a bit and then pinch and curve up the ends like a mustache. Pinch the center in just a little. When the cookie resembles a mustache, flatten the top again, place onto parchment-lined cookie sheet, and push a lollipop stick into the thickest section of the cookie.
4. Pop into the refrigerator to chill for 10 minutes. While the cookies are chilling, preheat the oven to 350°F.
5. Bake cookies for 12–15 minutes or until they are just starting to color. Allow to cool on cookie sheets until you can remove with a spatula to wire racks to finish cooling.

Christmas Tree Cookies

Makes 12 cookies

Instead of cut-out cookies this year, try this unusual and inspired technique for making swirly textured Christmas trees.

½ batch Play-Dough Cookies dough
¼ teaspoon green gel food color
¼ cup Royal Icing (see Chapter 9)
Large yellow star sprinkles
Red M&M's

1. Line 2 or 3 cookie sheets (depending on their size) with parchment paper.
2. Color the cookie dough green, kneading well.
3. Break off around 2 tablespoons of dough and roll into a long log about 8½" in length. Use the palms of your hands, not the fingertips, to get a smooth-looking finish. Place the log of dough on a parchment-lined cookie sheet.
4. Keeping the dough in one piece, without breaking or cutting, start making a Christmas tree (triangle) shape with about a 2" length for the bottom. Carefully bend the log in a tight U shape so that it is lying back flat on the parchment paper, parallel to the original length, touching it but not on top of it. Make this second course around 1½". Bend the dough back again, making a third course, which is parallel to the second and a little shorter.
5. Continue to bend the dough and make each course a little shorter, to make a long triangle shape. You should end with a pointed top. Repeat for remaining dough.

Insert a lollipop stick into the bottom of each Christmas tree, pushing the stick in about an inch.

6. Pop into the refrigerator to chill. While the cookies are chilling, preheat the oven to 350°F.

7. Bake cookies for 15 minutes or until they are just starting to turn golden around the edges. Allow to cool on cookie sheets until you can remove them with a spatula to wire racks to cool.

8. When the cookies are cool, place a little bit of Royal Icing into a Ziploc bag with a small hole cut in the corner. Use a bit of the icing to attach M&M's to look like ornaments. Attach a star (or one yellow M&M's candy) at the top of each tree.

♦ ♦ ♦

Jumbo Candy Canes

Makes 12 cookies

Love candy canes but don't love how sticky the kids get eating them? Solve the icky-sticky hand problem and make cookie candy cane treats this Christmas.

1 batch Play-Dough Cookies dough
½ teaspoon red gel food color

1. Line 2 or 3 cookie sheets (depending on their size) with parchment paper.

2. Divide the cookie dough into two pieces, and color one section red.

3. Break off 2½ tablespoons of red dough and roll into a long log about 6" long and ½" in diameter. Use the palms of your hands (not the fingertips) to get a smooth-looking finish. Repeat with the uncolored dough.

4. Twist the two colors together to look like a rope and then gently roll the two different-colored doughs together once again, using the palms of your hands, until you have a log around 7" in length.

5. Place the log on the parchment cookie sheet and bend the tip of the cookie over to resemble a candy cane. Repeat for the remaining dough. Insert a lollipop stick into the bottom of each "candy cane," pushing the stick in about an inch.

6. Pop into the refrigerator to chill. While the cookies are chilling, preheat the oven to 350°F.

7. Bake cookies for 15 minutes or until they are just starting to color. Allow to cool on cookie sheets until you can remove them with a spatula to wire racks to cool.

FOR PEPPERMINT CANDY CANES, MIX IN A TEASPOON OF PEPPERMINT EXTRACT WHEN YOU MAKE THE PLAY-DOUGH COOKIES RECIPE.

DECORATED COOKIES

Make these easy-to-mix cookie bases and then follow the instructions to whip up sensational decorated cookie creations using frosting, candies, and fondant.

The basic recipes provided all make 24 regular-sized cookies, but as cookie cutters are all different shapes and sizes sometimes it might make more or less. If you have dough left over, you can keep it wrapped in the fridge for 3 days or freeze it wrapped it plastic wrap in an airtight container for 4 weeks. Defrost it in the fridge when you are ready to make more cookies. Once baked and decorated, the cookies should be stored laying flat in airtight containers. Keep frosted cookies for up to 3 days and fondant decorated cookies for up to 5 days.

IF YOU ARE NOT REALLY A FAN OF ROLLING OUT COOKIE DOUGH, FOLLOW THIS EASY TIP: AFTER MIXING THE DOUGH, PLACE IT ON TOP OF A PIECE OF PARCHMENT PAPER, PLACE ANOTHER PIECE ON TOP, AND ROLL OUT TO THE DESIRED THICKNESS. THEN YOU CAN CHILL THE DOUGH UNTIL IT'S FIRM ENOUGH TO BE CUT INTO SHAPES. THE SCRAPS CAN BE KNEADED AND REROLLED IN THE SAME WAY.

Vanilla Sugar Cookies

Makes 2 dozen cookies

These easy-to-make and delicious sugar cookies are the perfect base for any of the decorated cookie recipes that follow. This recipe can easily be halved if you only want a batch of 12 cookies.

3 cups all-purpose flour
1 teaspoon baking powder
8 ounces (2 sticks) unsalted butter, room temperature
1 cup sugar
1 large egg
1 teaspoon vanilla extract

1. Line 2 or 3 cookie sheets (depending on their size) with parchment paper.
2. Sift together flour and baking powder. Set aside.
3. In a large bowl, using an electric mixer at high speed, cream butter and sugar until fluffy, around 3 minutes. Reduce speed to medium low, add egg and vanilla, and mix until combined. Reduce speed to low, add flour mixture, and mix well.
4. Refrigerate dough about 1 hour, or until firm enough to roll. If you leave the mixture too long, it may get very hard and need to soften a bit. If that happens, just let it sit out a little while, cut off sections, and knead them until you can roll the mixture out.
5. Using a lightly floured large rolling pin, roll out cookie dough on a lightly floured surface to about ¼" thickness. You can roll out only enough to cut one or two cookies if you have trouble rolling out large amounts.
6. Cut out desired shapes and place on parchment-lined cookie sheets. Gently push a lollipop stick into each cookie. To check the positioning of the sticks, place some parchment paper over the top of the cookies and top the paper with a cutting board. Holding the cookie sheet and the cutting board together like a sandwich, turn the cookies over and remove the parchment paper that originally lined the cookie sheet so you can see the backs. If any of the sticks are showing through, push a scrap of cookie dough over the top of the stick until it is covered. Replace the parchment paper and, using the same method, turn the cookies right-side up again.
7. You can knead the remaining scraps of dough and roll out again to cut more shapes until all dough is used or you have enough cookies.
8. Place cookies in fridge to chill for 30 minutes while you preheat the oven to 325°F.
9. Bake cookies until the middle is set and the edges are golden brown. Depending on the size of the cookies, it could take 10–20 minutes.
10. Leave on cookie sheet a few minutes and then use a spatula to remove to a wire baking rack to cool. Once cool, decorate as desired.

Rich Chocolate Sugar Cookies

Makes 2 dozen cookies

This cookie holds it shape very well as there is no baking powder. Use a dark, rich cocoa for the best super-chocolaty results. This recipe can easily be halved if you only want a batch of 12 cookies.

> 3 cups all-purpose flour
>
> ⅔ cup unsweetened cocoa
>
> 2 sticks (8 ounces) unsalted butter at room temperature
>
> 1½ cup superfine sugar (use regular granulated sugar if you can't locate superfine)
>
> 2 large eggs
>
> 2 teaspoon vanilla

1. Line 2 or 3 cookie sheets (depending on their size) with parchment paper.
2. Sift together flour and cocoa. Set aside.
3. In a large bowl, cream butter and sugar. Add eggs and vanilla and mix until well blended. Add flour and cocoa mixture and mix well.
4. Refrigerate dough until firm enough to roll (at least one hour). If you leave the mixture too long, it may get very hard and need to soften a bit. If that happens, just let it sit out a little while, cut off sections, and knead them until you can roll the mixture out.
5. Using a lightly floured large rolling pin, roll out cookie dough on a lightly floured surface to about ¼" thickness. You can roll out only enough to cut one or two cookies if you have trouble rolling out large amounts.
6. Cut out desired shapes and place on parchment-lined cookie sheets. Gently push a lollipop stick into each cookie. To check the positioning of the sticks, place some parchment paper over the top of the cookies and top the paper with a cutting board. Holding the cookie sheet and the cutting board together like a sandwich, turn the cookies over and remove the parchment paper that originally lined the cookie sheet so you can see the backs. If any of the sticks are showing through, push a scrap of cookie dough over the top of the stick until it is covered. Replace the parchment paper and, using the same method, turn the cookies right-side up again.
7. You can knead the remaining scraps of dough and roll out again to cut more shapes until all dough is used or you have enough cookies.
8. Place cookies in fridge to chill for 30 minutes while you preheat the oven to 325°F.
9. Bake cookies until the middle is set and they are cooked all the way through. Depending on the size of the cookies, it could take 10–20 minutes.
10. Leave on cookie sheet a few minutes and then use a spatula to remove to a wire baking rack to cool. Once cool, decorate as desired.

Gingerbread Cookies

Makes 2 dozen

These fragrant cookies will make the house smell wonderful when you open the oven door. You can make traditional gingerbread shapes or use this dough in place of the sugar cookie recipes to make any of the decorated cookies.

3 cups all-purpose flour

1 stick (4 ounces) unsalted butter at room temperature

2 teaspoons baking soda

½ teaspoon ground cloves

2 teaspoons ground ginger

2 teaspoons ground cinnamon

⅓ cup brown sugar, lightly packed

½ cup dark corn syrup

1 egg

1. Line 2 or 3 cookie sheets (depending on their size) with parchment paper.

2. Combine all ingredients in a bowl. Turn out on a lightly floured work surface and knead until smooth.

3. Refrigerate dough until firm enough to roll (at least one hour). If you leave the mixture too long, it may get very hard and need to soften a bit. If that happens, just let it sit out a little while, cut off sections, and knead them until you can roll the mixture out.

4. Using a large rolling pin, roll out cookie dough on a lightly floured surface to about ¼" thickness. You can roll out only enough to cut one or two cookies if you have trouble rolling out large amounts.

5. Cut out desired shapes and place on parchment-lined cookie sheets. Gently push a lollipop stick into each cookie. To check the positioning of the sticks, place some parchment paper over the top of the cookies and top the paper with a cutting board. Holding the cookie sheet and the cutting board together like a sandwich, turn the cookies over and remove the parchment paper that originally lined the cookie sheet so you can see the backs. If any of the sticks are showing through, push a scrap of cookie dough over the top of the stick until it is covered. Replace the parchment paper and, using the same method, turn the cookies right-side up again.

6. You can knead the remaining scraps of dough and roll out again to cut more shapes until all dough is used or you have enough cookies.

7. Place cookies in fridge to chill for 30 minutes while you preheat the oven to 325°F.

8. Bake for 10–12 minutes, depending on the size of the cookies, until lightly golden.

Traffic Light Cookies

Go! STOP! Go! Green, orange, and red candy combine to make simple Traffic Light Cookies, which are truckloads of fun and delicious to boot. Any type of candy will do as long as they are the same shape—round—and the right colors.

> 1 batch Vanilla Sugar Cookies or Rich Chocolate Sugar Cookies dough made using a 2" round cookie cutter
>
> 2 cups white frosting (use store bought frosting for a really white color or you can use the Vanilla Buttercream Frosting from Chapter 2)
>
> 24 round red candies
>
> 24 round green candies
>
> 24 round orange candies

1. Once cookies are cool, spread the frosting over the entire top of the cookie with a knife. Press on colored candy to look like traffic lights with red at the top, then orange, and then green at the bottom.
2. Place on cookie sheets until the frosting has had a chance to set, and then store in airtight containers.

Traffic Light
Cookies

Touchdown Cookie Pops

The kids will score points if they make these sweet football snacks to munch on while watching the game.

1 batch Rich Chocolate Sugar Cookies made using a football-shaped cookie cutter

1½ batches Chocolate Buttercream Frosting (see Chapter 2)

½ batch Royal Icing (see Chapter 9)

1. Once cookies are cool, use a flat knife to spread chocolate frosting over the whole top of the cookie.
2. Spoon the Royal Icing into a Ziploc bag. Pipe a long line near the top of the football shape and then shorter lines crossing the long line to look like the stitching on a football. Pipe a half circle from the top of the cookie to the bottom, about ¾" from each side.
3. Place on cookie sheets to allow the Royal Icing to set, and then store in an airtight container.

Touchdown Cookie Pops

Sweet Spring Flower Cookies

Wind green ribbon around the lollipop sticks so they look like stems and pop a bunch into a pretty vase to make a gorgeous spring display. For a bit of variety you can color the frosting pink or yellow.

1 batch Vanilla Sugar Cookies or Rich Chocolate Sugar Cookies made using a 3" daisy-shaped cookie cutter

2 batches Vanilla Buttercream Frosting (see Chapter 2)

M&M's Minis

1. Once cookies are cool, spread the buttercream frosting over the entire top of the cookie with a knife. Press one M&M's Minis candy into the center of each cookie and surround with 6 M&M's Minis, all the same color, to make "petals." Place contrasting M&M's onto each petal.
2. Place on cookie sheets until the buttercream frosting has had a chance to set, and then store in airtight containers for up to 3 days.

Cute and Kooky Face Cookies

Bake the cookies, lay out the frosting and candy, and have a decorating party. A good idea when you're dealing with a group of kids is to provide a separate cookie sheet or large plate lined with parchment paper for holding each child's finished cookies. Write his or her name in the corner of the sheet, and at the end it will be easy to tell which cookies belong to which kid.

1 batch Vanilla Sugar Cookies or Rich Chocolate Sugar Cookies made using a 3" round cookie cutter

2 batches Vanilla Buttercream Frosting (see Chapter 2)

Jelly beans, Skittles, mini marshmallows, M&M's, red licorice, Froot Loops cereal

1. Place the candy in small dishes on a table.
2. Use a knife to spread the white frosting over the entire top of each cookie. Allow the kids to decorate the faces with the candy however they like, trying to make the funniest face they can by using candy pieces for eyes, nose, mouth, ears, and hair.
3. Place on cookie sheets until the buttercream frosting has had a chance to set, and then store in airtight containers.

Dino Stomp Cookies

Stomp Stomp Stomp . . . Roar! The dinosaurs are coming—better eat them up quick before they eat you. The dinos in the recipe are made with green frosting, but purple, orange, or blue with contrasting candy would also look great.

- 1 batch Vanilla Sugar Cookies or Rich Chocolate Sugar Cookies dough made using a dinosaur-shaped cookie cutter
- 2 batches Vanilla Buttercream Frosting (see Chapter 2) with a few drops of green food color added
- Yellow and orange Reese's Pieces
- Yellow and orange M&M's Minis
- Yellow and orange sprinkles
- Premade edible sugar eyes

1. Once cookies are cool, spread the green frosting over the entire top of the cookie with a knife. Place two of the Reese's Pieces onto the back of the dinosaur to make large spots, and then push some of the M&M's Minis in around to look like smaller spots on the dinosaur's back and neck. Place a couple of the yellow and orange sprinkles along the tail to look like spikes, and finish off with an eye.
2. Place on cookie sheets until the buttercream frosting has had a chance to set, and then store in airtight containers.

Dino Stomp Cookies

Twinkle
Star Pops

Blast-Off
Rocket
Cookies

Blast-Off Rocket Cookies

It will be a countdown to fun with everyone having a blast decorating and playing with these fun space-themed cookies.

1 batch Vanilla Sugar Cookies or Rich Chocolate Sugar Cookies dough made using a rocket cookie cutter

2 batches Vanilla Buttercream Frosting (see Chapter 2) with a few drops of blue gel food color added

Blue M&M's

Red sprinkles

1. Line 2 or 3 cookie sheets (depending on their size) with parchment paper.
2. Cut a strip of parchment paper 2½" to 3" wide so that when you lay it on top of a rocket cookie you can see ½" to ¾" at both the top and bottom. The recommended parchment paper strip is based on a rocket cookie cutter 4" high, so if your cutter is a different size, trim the paper as required.
3. Once cookies are cool, spread the frosting over the entire top of the cookie with a knife. Lay the paper strip across the middle of the cookie so you can see the peaked top and bottom rocket thrusters. Scatter red sprinkles generously over the top and bottom sections and press on lightly. Carefully remove the parchment paper.
4. Stick 3 blue M&M's in a straight line in between the red top and bottom sections.
5. Place on cookie sheets until the frosting has had a chance to set, and then store in airtight containers.

Wizard Wands

Encourage active minds to engage in interactive and imaginative play with these magical-themed wand cookies. You can easily turn these wands into princess wands by coloring the frosting pink and using purple and pink candy decorations. Wizard or princess wands look great with long lengths of twirly ribbon tied to the lollipop sticks.

1 batch Vanilla Sugar Cookies or Rich Chocolate Sugar Cookies made with a 3" star-shaped cookie cutter

2 batches Vanilla Buttercream Frosting (see Chapter 2) with ¼ teaspoon blue gel food coloring added

Blue M&M's Minis

Gold or silver sprinkles

1. Once cookies are cool, spread the buttercream frosting over the entire top of the cookie with a knife. Press on some blue M&M's and lightly cover with the sprinkles.
2. Place on cookie sheets until the buttercream frosting has had a chance to set, and then store in airtight containers.

Big Ear Bunny Cookies

Bunny cookie cutters are easy to find around Easter; at other times of the year you may need to check out a specialty cake supply store. You can use brown M&M's in place of the pre-made sugar eyes if you like.

1 batch Vanilla Sugar Cookies or Rich Chocolate Sugar
   Cookies made using a bunny face cookie cutter
4 large marshmallows
Pink sanding sugar
4 cups store bought white frosting
Pink M&M's Minis
Premade sugar eye decorations
Red Twizzlers candy cut into twenty-four 1" pieces

1. To make the bunny ears, use safety scissors to cut the corners off the marshmallows, making shapes about 1½" by ¼". Pour out a couple of tablespoons of sanding sugar into a shallow dish and press the sticky side of each marshmallow piece into the sugar. Set aside.

2. Once the cookies are cool, spread the frosting over the entire top of the cookie with a knife. Press on a pink M&M's Minis candy for a nose, add the premade eyes, and the red Twizzlers mouth. Stick the marshmallow ears in the center of the cookie ear sections, with the pink sanding sugar facing outward.

3. Leave on cookie sheets until the frosting has had a chance to set and then store in airtight containers.

POP TIP

MAKE PINK BUNNIES BY TINTING THE FROSTING PINK AND LEAVING THE MARSHMALLOW EARS WHITE BY OMITTING THE PINK SANDING SUGAR STEP.

Big Ear Bunny Cookies

No need for special cookie cutters when you make these cool cookie pops. If you don't want to frost the cookies, try coloring the dough with gel food color.

1 batch Vanilla Sugar Cookies or Rich Chocolate Sugar Cookie dough

2 batches Vanilla or Chocolate Buttercream Frosting (see Chapter 2)

Candy for decorating, like M&M's or jelly beans

1. Line 2 or 3 cookie sheets (depending on their size) with parchment paper.
2. Roll out the cookie dough. Have children place their hands lightly onto the rolled-out dough and lightly trace around the outline of their hands with a skewer or lollipop stick. Older kids can do their own, and you can help the younger children. Use a knife to cut around the outline to make hand-shaped cookies. Carefully lift the cookies and place them onto the prepared cookie sheets. Gently push a lollipop stick into each cookie. To check the positioning of the sticks, place some parchment paper over the top of the cookies and top the paper with a cutting board. Holding the cookie sheet and the cutting board together like a sandwich, turn the cookies over and remove the parchment paper that originally lined the cookie sheet so you can see the backs. If any of the sticks are showing through, push a scrap of cookie dough over the top of the stick until it is covered. Pop the cookie cut-outs into the fridge to chill for 30 minutes.
3. Heat oven to 350°F while cookies are chilling.
4. Bake cookies for 12–16 minutes or until golden. If the cookies are not baking evenly, turn the cookie sheets around halfway through baking.
5. Remove from oven and cool on cookie sheets for 5 minutes or until you can lift the cookie up with a spatula without the lollipop stick being disturbed. Place onto wire rack to cool completely.
6. Once cookies are cool, use a flat knife to spread chocolate frosting over the whole top of the cookie. If you like, you can use candy for the nails or just decorate the whole cookie with random candy.
7. Leave on cookie sheets until the buttercream frosting has had a chance to set, and then store in airtight containers for up to 3 days.

Spooky Ghost Cookies

Spooky and delicious ghost cookies will have the kids running around trying to scare anyone in their path. Frosting from the supermarket is whiter than homemade buttercream, so if you want those ghosts to gleam, try the store-bought stuff.

1 batch Vanilla Sugar Cookies or Rich Chocolate Sugar Cookies made using a ghost-shaped cookie cutter

4 cups store-bought white frosting

Black confetti sprinkles, M&M's Minis, or premade sugar eyes

1. Once cookies are cool, spread the frosting over the entire top of the cookie with a knife. Add eyes using the black confetti pieces, sugar eyes, or M&M's Minis.
2. Leave on cookie sheets until the frosting has had a chance to set and then store in airtight containers.

Totally Batty Cookies

Totally tantalizing. Spreading the frosting around the bat wings can get a little tricky, but that's okay. If you have any problems, just scrape it off and start again. If you don't have chocolate jimmies, you can used finely crushed Oreo cookies, grated chocolate, or leave the frosting plain.

1 batch Rich Chocolate Sugar Cookies made using a bat-shaped cookie cutter

2 batches Chocolate Buttercream Frosting (see Chapter 2)

Yellow or red M&M's Minis or premade sugar eyes

Chocolate jimmies

1. Once cookies are cool, spread the frosting over the entire top of the cookie with a knife. Add the yellow or red candy or ready-made eyes for eyes. Sprinkle cookies with the chocolate jimmies and lightly press down onto the frosting.
2. Place on cookie sheets until the frosting has had a chance to set, and then store in airtight containers.

Spooky
Ghost
and Totally
Batty
Cookies

MARSHMALLOW FONDANT DECORATED COOKIES

Fondant-covered cookies seem like they would be difficult to make as they look so perfectly pretty, but the technique is similar to playing with Play-Doh, and we all know how great kids are at that! A recipe for Marshmallow Fondant can be found in Chapter 9. Fondant must be kept wrapped and in an airtight container so it does not dry out. If it becomes hard to work with, try heating the fondant in the microwave for a few seconds, in 5-second bursts at high, and then knead, adding in a very small amount of Crisco or other vegetable shortening if required.

◆◆◆

Valentine Sweetheart Cookie Pops

Let your cookie pops do the talking and make up a batch of sweet-talking treats in hues of pink, white, and red.

1 batch **Vanilla Sugar Cookies** or **Rich Chocolate Sugar Cookies** made with a heart-shaped cookie cutter

1 batch **pink Marshmallow Fondant** (see Chapter 9)

Cornstarch for dusting

1 batch **Royal Icing** (see Chapter 9)

Premade sugar flowers

Edible pen—pink or red

1. Knead the Marshmallow Fondant until pliable, and break off a large handful to work with. Cover the remainder with plastic wrap and place in an airtight container or Ziploc bag.
2. Dust the work surface with a little sifted cornstarch and roll out the pink Marshmallow Fondant to ⅛" thickness. Lift the fondant and turn it as you would a pie crust, dusting with more cornstarch underneath if required to keep it from sticking. Cut out heart shapes using the cookie cutter and adhere them to the cookies using a small amount of water brushed onto the cookie. If necessary, use a small rolling pin to push the fondant out to the edges by lightly rolling it over the fondant-covered cookie.
3. Place the Royal Icing in a piping bag with a plain tip or in a Ziploc bag with a small hole cut out the corner. With the cookies on a flat surface, pipe dots all around the heart about ¼" in from the edge. Secure a couple of sugar flowers in the corner of each cookie with some of the Royal Icing.
4. Leave the cookies to set for a couple of hours. Then using the foodsafe edible pen, write sweet comments like "love you" and "be mine."

YOU'RE CUTE

BE MINE

LOVE YOU

Valentine
Sweetheart
Cookie Pops

These simple-looking cookies are visually appealing—who doesn't love the look of a cute button? If you're having trouble finding a second cutter that's a smaller size than the first, try checking out small drinking glasses around the house as well as other foodsafe circle shapes that might do the trick.

1 batch Vanilla Sugar Cookies or Rich Chocolate Sugar Cookies made with a 2¼" round cookie cutter

1 batch Marshmallow Fondant (see Chapter 9)

1 batch Marshmallow Fondant (see Chapter 9) colored either blue, red, or purple

Cornstarch for dusting
Round cookie cutters, 2¼" and 2"

1. Knead the Marshmallow Fondant until pliable, and break off a large handful to work with. Cover the remainder with plastic wrap and place in an airtight container or Ziploc bag.

2. Dust the work surface with a little sifted cornstarch and roll out the fondant to ⅛" thickness. Lift the fondant and turn it as you would a pie crust, dusting with more cornstarch underneath if required to keep it from sticking. Cut out round shapes using the cookie cutter and adhere them to the cookies using a small amount of water brushed onto the cookie. If necessary, use a small rolling pin to push the fondant out to the edges by lightly rolling it over the fondant-covered cookie.

3. Take the second smaller cutter and lightly push down to make a circle indent just inside the cookie. It should look like the rim around a button.

4. Using the end of a lollipop stick, lightly press down to make 4 hole indents in a square shape at the center of the cookie to look like the holes of a button.

Big Button Cookies

Howdy Partner! Mosey on over and check out this neat stamping technique for decorating cookies. It's child's play once you get the hang of it.

> 1 batch 3" round Vanilla Sugar Cookies or Rich Chocolate Sugar Cookies
>
> 1 batch Marshmallow Fondant (see Chapter 9) (¾ white and ¼ light blue)
>
> Cornstarch for dusting
>
> 3" round cookie cutter
>
> Small brush and water
>
> Sheriff stamp
>
> Blue gel food color (or edible pen)
>
> 1½" star cutter

1. Knead the blue Marshmallow Fondant until pliable, and break off a section. Cover the remainder with plastic wrap and place in an airtight container or Ziploc bag.

2. Dust the work surface with a little sifted cornstarch and roll out the blue Marshmallow Fondant to ⅛" thickness. Lift the fondant and turn it as you would a pie crust, dusting with more cornstarch underneath if required to keep it from sticking. Cut out 12 star shapes and lay them onto parchment paper to dry a little.

3. Knead the white Marshmallow Fondant until pliable, and break off a handful to work with. Cover the remainder with plastic wrap and place in an airtight container or Ziploc bag.

4. Dust the work surface with a little sifted cornstarch quickly knead the white Marshmallow Fondant and roll out a portion to about ⅛" thickness. Lift the fondant and turn it as you would a pie crust, dusting with more cornstarch underneath if required to keep it from sticking. Using the round cookie cutter, cut out a round and adhere it to the cookie by lightly brushing it with water and then pressing the Marshmallow Fondant down gently. If necessary, use the small rolling pin to push the fondant out to the edges by lightly rolling it over the fondant-covered cookie. Repeat with the remaining fondant.

5. Pop a little bit of blue gel food color onto a clean new paint brush and lightly brush the sheriff stamp with food color. Stamp onto the middle of each blue star. The kids might like to practice this a few times on some paper.

6. Once the blue stars are stamped, attach them to the middle of the white cookies with a very small amount of water. Leave lying down to dry and set for 10 minutes.

Cowboy Hat Cookie Pops

Yeehaw! Round up the kids and start working on these Western-theme cookie pops. If you do not have an edible pen, you can either leave the edge of the cookie plain or, before the fondant sets, use a toothpick to mark holes at even intervals to look like stitches.

> 1 batch Vanilla Sugar Cookies or Rich Chocolate Sugar Cookies made with a cowboy hat cookie cutter
>
> 1 batch Marshmallow Fondant (see Chapter 9) (¾ colored light blue, ⅛ colored red, and ⅛ white)
>
> Cornstarch for dusting
>
> Small star cutter or star-shaped sprinkles
>
> Edible pen—black

1. Knead the light blue Marshmallow Fondant until pliable, and break off a handful to work with. Cover the remainder with plastic wrap and place in an airtight container or Ziploc bag.

2. Dust the work surface with a little sifted cornstarch and roll out the blue Marshmallow Fondant to ⅛" thickness. Lift the fondant and turn it as you would a pie crust, dusting with more cornstarch underneath if required to keep it from sticking. Cut out cowboy hat shapes using the cookie cutter and adhere them to the cookies using a small amount of water brushed onto the cookie. If necessary, use a small rolling pin to push the fondant out to the edges by lightly rolling it over the fondant-covered cookie.

3. Repeat for remaining cookies.

4. Quickly knead and then roll out on a cornstarch dusted work surface the white Marshmallow Fondant to about ⅛" thick. Using a pizza cutter or knife, cut a long thin strip around ¼" in width to use as a hatband. Measure across the hat with a piece of string and then cut the white stripe with a knife to the length of the string. Adhere the fondant hatband to the cookie by lightly brushing it with a really tiny amount of water and then pressing the fondant down gently onto the hat. Repeat for all remaining cookies.

5. On the cornstarch-dusted work surface, quickly knead and then roll out the red fondant as thin as you can and cut out 12 stars. Adhere one star to each cookie with the tiniest amount of water. If you don't have a star cutter, use star-shaped sprinkles.

6. Leave the cookies to set for a couple of hours and then, using the food-safe edible pen, draw fake stitching all around the edge of the hat. Do not draw the stitches over the white band.

Cowboy Hat
Cookie Pops

Star cookies look great at a party mixed in with the New Sheriff in Town cookies or on their own for younger kids while you sing your favorite starry nursery rhymes together.

1 batch Vanilla Sugar Cookies or Rich Chocolate Sugar Cookies made with a 3" round cookie cutter

1 batch Marshmallow Fondant (see Chapter 9) (¾ light blue and ¼ dark blue)

Cornstarch for dusting

3" round cookie cutter

Small brush and water

Small star cutter, ejector type (if you don't have a small cutter, use star-shaped sprinkles or candy and a little royal icing)

1. Knead the Marshmallow Fondant until pliable, and break off a section. Cover the remainder with plastic wrap and place in an airtight container or Ziploc bag.

2. Dust the work surface with a little sifted cornstarch and roll out the light blue Marshmallow Fondant to about ⅛" thickness. Using the round cookie cutter, cut out a round and adhere it to a cookie by lightly brushing it with water and then pressing the Marshmallow Fondant down gently. If necessary, use the small rolling pin to push the fondant out to the edges by lightly rolling it over the fondant covered cookie. Repeat with the remaining fondant.

3. Quickly knead and then roll out on a cornstarch dusted work surface the darker blue fondant as thin as you can on the work surface. Using a small star cutter, cut out as many small stars as you can. Using a very small amount of water, attach the stars onto the white cookies in any pattern you like. Leave lying down to dry and set for 10 minutes.

USE RED, WHITE, AND BLUE FONDANT AND TURN THESE POPS INTO A PATRIOTIC TREAT!

Bring out your little one's inner artist with these draw-your-own cookies. This recipe makes a great party or play date activity, and everyone can take home their own special artwork treats afterward. Make sure you get pictures, though, as the art won't last forever.

1 batch **Vanilla Sugar Cookies** or **Rich Chocolate Sugar Cookies** made using the square cookie cutter specified below and wooden craft sticks

1 batch **Marshmallow Fondant** (see Chapter 9)

Cornstarch for dusting

Square cookie cutter about 3" × 3" (if not available use 3" round)

Edible food color paint (buy edible food paint or make your own using the Edible Paint recipe in Chapter 9)

1. Knead the Marshmallow Fondant until pliable, and break off a hanful to work with. Cover the remainder with plastic wrap and place in an airtight container or Ziploc bag.

2. Dust the work surface with a little sifted cornstarch and roll out a portion of the white Marshmallow Fondant to about ⅛" thick. Using the cookie cutter, cut out a square and adhere it to the cookie by lightly brushing it with water and then pressing the Marshmallow Fondant down gently. If necessary, use the small rolling pin to push the fondant out to the edges by lightly rolling it over the fondant-covered cookie. Repeat with the remaining cookies.

3. Leave the fondant-covered cookies uncovered overnight to set. If it is humid, it may take a little longer.

4. Put out dishes of edible paint, provide a paint brush for each child, and let them decorate as they like.

5. Leave the cookies on wire racks until dry and then store in an airtight container for up to 5 days.

FOR A LESS MESSY OPTION, BUY A PACKAGE OF EDIBLE FOOD WRITERS AND LET THE KIDS DRAW PICTURES ONTO THE COOKIES WITH THE MARKERS.

Candy Swirl
Cookie Pops

Classic shaped candy cookie treats look amazing, and you can make them in any color of the rainbow. For a sparkly finish you can sprinkle sanding sugar onto the Royal Icing swirl before it has had a chance to dry. Once set, just brush off the excess with a dry brush and voilà—sparkly sugar candy swirls. The cookie cutter used in this recipe is sometimes sold under the name of "wrapped candy," "hard candy," or "peppermint candy" cutter.

1 batch Vanilla Sugar Cookies or Rich Chocolate Sugar Cookies made using the candy-shaped cookie cutter described below

1 batch Marshmallow Fondant (see Chapter 9) (½ pink and ½ white)

Cornstarch for dusting

Candy-shaped cookie cutter (Preferred cutter to resemble a wrapped round hard candy with paper wrapper twisted at each end)

1 batch Royal Icing (see Chapter 9)

1. Knead the white Marshmallow Fondant until pliable, and break off a handful to work with. Cover the remainder with plastic wrap and place in an airtight container or Ziploc bag.

2. Dust the work surface with a little cornstarch and roll out the fondant to ⅛" thickness. Lift the fondant and turn it as you would a pie crust, dusting with more cornstarch underneath if required to keep it from sticking. Using the candy-shaped cookie cutter, cut out fondant shapes.

3. Repeat the process for the pink fondant so that you have 2 wrapped candy shapes in pink and white. Lie the white wrapped candy shape on top of the pink shape, and then using a plastic knife cut down on the shape where the hard candy round would meet the paper twist so that you are left with a round center and the 2 ends that resemble the paper twist ties.

4. Brush the cookies lightly with a little water and adhere a pink fondant round center candy shape to the center of the cookie and the white end paper tie shapes on the edges of the cookie. Use the small rolling pin to push the fondant out to the edges by lightly rolling over the fondant-covered cookie and then rub back and forth until the joins where the pink and white fondant meet are hard to see. Repeat for all the cookies.

5. Place the Royal Icing into a piping bag with a plain tip or a Ziploc bag with a small hole cut in the corner. Pipe a swirl on round center of each candy cookie pop, starting in the middle and working out. Leave cookies to set before storing.

Math Pop Quiz Cookies

1 + 1 = learning and delicious fun when you make these cookies. Use them to teach young kids how to add, with a cookie as a special treat at the end of each session for a job well done.

1 batch Vanilla Sugar Cookies or Rich Chocolate Sugar Cookies made using a 3" round cookie cutter

1 batch Marshmallow Fondant (see Chapter 9)
   (¾ white, ¼ red, ¼ blue)

Cornstarch for dusting
Number and plus-sign cutters

1. Knead the Marshmallow Fondant until pliable, and break off a handful to work with. Cover the remainder with plastic wrap and place in an airtight container or Ziploc bag.

2. Dust the work surface with a little sifted cornstarch and roll out the white fondant to ⅛" thickness. Lift the fondant and turn it as you would a pie crust, dusting with more cornstarch underneath if required to keep it from sticking. Cut out round shapes using the cookie cutter and adhere them to the cookies using a small amount of water brushed onto the cookie. If necessary, use a small rolling pin to push the fondant out to the edges by lightly rolling it over the fondant-covered cookie.

3. Take the colored Marshmallow Fondant, knead it quickly, and roll out to about ⅛" thick. Cut out numbers using the cookie cutters and adhere numbers to the cookie by lightly brushing them with a really tiny amount of water and then pressing the Marshmallow Fondant down gently. Repeat for remaining cookies.

4. Place on cookie sheets until the fondant and water has a chance to set, and then store in airtight containers.

◆ ◆ ◆

FlutterBelle Cookie Pops

Pink and purple butterflies with sugar—what an awesome combination! No puppy dogs tails here; these cookies are made for the little girl in us all. You can make the sugar butterflies by following the instructions in the Butterfly Kisses cake pop recipe (Chapter 2) or just buy premade sugar butterflies.

1 batch Vanilla Sugar Cookies, made using a 3" blossom cookie cutter

1½" round cutter

1 batch Marshmallow Fondant (see Chapter 9) (⅜ light pink, ⅜ light purple, and ¼ white)

Cornstarch for dusting
Sugar butterflies
½ cup Royal Icing (see Chapter 9)

1. Knead the Marshmallow Fondant until pliable, and break off a section. Cover the remainder with plastic wrap and place in an airtight container or Ziploc bag.

2. Dust the work surface with a little cornstarch. Break off a piece of the light pink fondant and roll out, using a small rolling pin, until ⅛" thick. Lift the fondant and turn it as you would a pie crust, dusting with more cornstarch underneath if required to keep it from sticking. Using the 3" flower cutter, cut out fondant flower shapes.

3. Brush the cookies lightly with a little water and adhere the flower fondant shapes using the small rolling pin, gently pressing down. If necessary, use the small rolling pin to push the fondant out to the edges by lightly rolling it over the fondant-covered cookie. Repeat for half the cookies.

4. Roll out the light purple fondant and cut out the 3" flower shapes, adhering them to the remaining cookies with water as described in the previous steps.

5. Knead and roll out the white fondant. Cut out 1½" circles and adhere them to the center of the flowers using a tiny amount of water.

6. Place the Royal Icing into a small Ziploc bag and cut a tiny hole from the corner. Use the Royal Icing to adhere the butterflies to the center of each blossom. Lay the cookies on cookie sheets to set.

FlutterBelle
Cookie Pops

Lollipop Cookie Pops

Get the kids to practice the coiling technique with Play-Doh if you like before they start on the fondant. They'll be fondant-coiling experts in no time.

> 1 batch Vanilla Sugar Cookies, made using 3½" round cookie cutter
>
> 1½ batches Marshmallow Fondant (½ red and ½ white)
>
> Cornstarch for dusting
>
> Water and brush

1. Knead the Marshmallow Fondant until pliable and divide each color into 12 even sections. Take once piece of each color and cover the remainder and store in a Ziploc bag. Roll one piece of fondant between the palms of your hands and the work surface to make a long, even rope about ½" in diameter. Repeat with other color.
2. Twist the two colors together to look like a rope and then gently roll the two different-colored doughs together once again, using the palms of your hands, until you have an even rope ½" in diameter.
3. Brush the round cookie pop lightly with water. Starting in the middle of the cookie, coil the twisted rope of fondant around like a snail. Gently press down the coil with the palm of your hand to secure the fondant to the cookie. If needed, you can press down lightly to push the fondant out to the edge of the cookie. Repeat for remaining cookies.
4. Place on cookie sheets to set overnight.

POP TIP

YOU CAN MIX IT UP AND USE MORE THAN TWO FONDANT COLORS, OR A DIFFERENT RATIO THAN HALF AND HALF; IN ANY CASE, YOU WILL NEED AROUND 3 OUNCES OF MARSHMALLOW FONDANT IN TOTAL FOR EACH COOKIE.

◆ ◆ ◆

Cute-as-a-Button Blossom Cookie Pops

Honestly, buttons just make everything look cuter! Made to emulate scrapbook crafts, these cookies would look extra inspired with some fake stitching drawn around the edge with edible pen. The kids will have a great time making fun patterns in the petals with the toothpick.

> 1 batch Vanilla Sugar Cookies or Rich Chocolate Sugar Cookies made using a 3" flower or blossom cookie cutter
>
> Smaller round cutter, about 1"
>
> 1 batch Marshmallow Fondant (see Chapter 9) (¾ pink and ¼ purple)
>
> Cornstarch for dusting
>
> Water and small brush

1. Knead the bright pink Marshmallow Fondant until pliable. Break off a large handful to work with. Cover the remainder with plastic wrap and place in an airtight container or Ziploc bag.

2. Dust the work surface with a little sifted cornstarch and roll out the pink Marshmallow Fondant to ⅛" thickness. Lift the fondant and turn it as you would a pie crust, dusting with more cornstarch underneath if required to keep it from sticking. Using the 3" flower cutter, cut out fondant flower shapes.

3. Brush the cookies lightly with a little water and adhere the flower fondant shapes using the small rolling pin, gently pressing down. Repeat for all the cookies.

4. Knead the bright purple fondant until pliable, roll out on a cornstarch dusted worktop to ⅛" thickness, and cut out 1" circles and adhere them to the center of the flowers using a tiny amount of water. Using the flat end of a toothpick, make 4 holes in each to represent button holes.

5. Use the toothpick to make decorative patterns on the flower petals.

6. If you like, you can use a little of the remaining pink fondant to make "string" in the button holes. To do this, roll the fondant between your fingers and the work surface to make thin logs, and them cut them to desired length with a sharp knife. Adhere to buttons with the smallest amount of water.

Cute-as-a-Button Blossom Cookie Pops

Head out on a safari and see if you can catch some of these cookies. A simple pattern packs a huge impact and turns a mask into a cool jungle costume.

> 1 batch Vanilla Sugar Cookies or Rich Chocolate Sugar Cookies made using a mask-shaped cookie cutter with wooden craft stick instead of lollipop stick
>
> 1½ batches Marshmallow Fondant (see Chapter 9) (⅓ white, ⅓ orange, ⅙ black, ⅙ brown)
>
> Cornstarch for dusting
>
> Small oval cutter, about 1" × ¾"
>
> Small brush and water

1. When you remove the cookies from the oven, work quickly using the small oval cutter on both the eye cut-out sections of the mask to make the area even (the cookie dough will have spread during the baking process.) Cool on cookie sheets for 5 minutes or until you can lift the cookie up with a spatula without the wooden craft stick being disturbed. Place onto wire rack to cool completely.

2. Knead the Marshmallow Fondant until pliable, and break off a section. Cover the remainder with plastic wrap and place in an airtight container or Ziploc bag.

3. Dust the work surface with a little sifted cornstarch and roll out the white fondant to ⅛" thickness. Lift the fondant and turn it as you would a pie crust, dusting with more cornstarch underneath if required to keep it from sticking. Cut out mask shapes using the cookie cutter and adhere them to the cookies using a small amount of water brushed onto each cookie. Cover 6 cookies with

Safari Mask Cookies

white fondant. If necessary, use the small rolling pin to push the fondant out to the edges by lightly rolling over the fondant-covered cookie. Use a knife to even up any over hand taking extra care around the eye area.

4. Repeat the process to cover 6 cookies in orange fondant.

5. Take the black Marshmallow Fondant and roll out to about ⅛" thickness. Using a knife, cut out uneven stripes around ¼" at their widest to resemble zebra stripes and adhere them to the cookies. If necessary, carefully use a little bit of water to make them adhere. The black fondant will bleed onto the white if you use too much water, so have absorbent paper ready to wipe any excess. Repeat for remaining white cookies.

6. Break off very small pieces of the brown fondant, about the size of a pea, and press them out into uneven shapes. The spots should resemble animal spots like a giraffe pelt. Adhere to the cookies using a tiny amount of water.

7. Place on cookie sheets until the fondant and water have a chance to set, and then store in airtight containers.

Beautiful Butterfly Wand Cookie Pops

The kids will delight in making these butterfly wands flutter from flower to flower. Tie long pink and purple ribbons to the lollipop sticks after you have decorated the cookies to make the wands appear extra swirly.

1 batch Vanilla Sugar Cookies or Rich Chocolate Sugar Cookies made using a butterfly-shaped cookie cutter

1 batch pink Marshmallow Fondant (see Chapter 9)

Cornstarch for dusting

1 batch Royal Icing (see Chapter 9)

Skittles or M&M's

1. Line 2 or 3 cookie sheets (depending on their size) with parchment paper.

2. Knead the pink Marshmallow Fondant until pliable, and break off a large handful. Cover the remainder with plastic wrap and place in an airtight container or Ziploc bag.

3. Dust the work surface with a little sifted cornstarch and roll out the fondant to ⅛" thickness. Lift the fondant and turn it as you would a pie crust, dusting with more cornstarch underneath if required to keep it from sticking. Cut out butterfly shapes using the cookie cutter and adhere them to the cookies using a small amount of water brushed onto the cookie. If necessary, use a small rolling pin to push the fondant out to the edges by lightly rolling it over the fondant-covered cookie.

4. Repeat for remaining cookies.

5. Spoon the Royal Icing into a Ziploc bag and cut a small hole out of one corner. Use the icing to decorate the butterfly cookies with dots on the wings. Pipe a line of Royal Icing in the center of each butterfly and place 4 or 5 Skittles or M&M's in a line to look like the butterfly's body. If you like, add some more candy to the wings for decoration.

6. Place on cookie sheets until the fondant and Royal Icing have a chance to set. Tie long lengths of ribbon at the top of the stick where the cookie meets the stick. Store cookies in airtight containers.

This cloud cookie is made by using a metal blossom cookie cutter and squashing it into a cloud shape. If you are not going to use the cloud shape a lot, you can press it back and make it into a blossom cutter again. These clouds look super served with the Over the Rainbow Cookies.

1 batch Vanilla Sugar Cookies or Rich Chocolate Sugar Cookies made with a 2½" metal blossom cookie cutter (or cloud cutter)

1 batch Marshmallow Fondant (see Chapter 9)

Cornstarch for dusting

1 batch Royal Icing (see Chapter 9)

Water and small brush

1. Knead the Marshmallow Fondant until pliable, and break off a section. Cover the remainder with plastic wrap and place in an airtight container or Ziploc bag.

2. Dust the work surface with a little sifted cornstarch and roll out the Marshmallow Fondant to ⅛" thickness. Lift the fondant and turn it as you would a pie crust, dusting with more cornstarch underneath if required to keep it from sticking. Cut out cloud shapes using the cutter.

3. Brush the cookies lightly with a little water and adhere the cloud fondant shapes, using the small rolling pin and gently pressing down. If necessary, use a small rolling pin to push the fondant out to the edges by lightly rolling it over the fondant-covered cookie. Repeat for all cookies.

4. Fill a clean Ziploc bag with Royal Icing and cut a small hole out of the corner. Pipe a line around the edge of the clouds about ¼" in from the edge. Lay the cookies down and allow Royal Icing to set.

POP TIP

IF YOU LIKE, SPRINKLE WHITE OR BLUE SANDING SUGAR ON THE COOKIES BEFORE THE ROYAL ICING SETS. AFTER THE ICING HAS SET, BRUSH EXCESS SUGAR AWAY WITH A DRY, CLEAN BRUSH.

CHAPTER 5

Outside-the-Box Pops

A collection of mouth-watering sweets on a stick that don't fit the normal constraints. From Oreo Truffle Pops to Hot Chocolate on a Stick, you're sure to find something innovative to tempt your taste buds in this section.

Popcorn
Balls

Popcorn Balls

Makes 12 balls

These super yummy balls of popcorn can be made even more delicious by adding ¾ cup of candy like Reese's Pieces when mixing the popcorn into the marshmallow mixture.

1 cup mini marshmallows

1 teaspoon water

4 tablespoons butter

⅓ cup corn syrup

10 cups popcorn

1¼ cups powdered sugar

Vegetable shortening, so you can work easily with the popcorn balls

12 lollipop sticks

1. Line a tray with parchment paper.
2. Place marshmallows, water, butter, and cornsyrup together in a large microwave-safe bowl and heat at high for 1 minute. Remove and stir and return to cook for a further 1 minute; stir until marshmallows are dissolved. Mix in popcorn and powdered sugar until completely combined.
3. Cover hands generously with vegetable shortening. Take handfuls of mixture and squash into a ball shape, continue until all mixture is used. Should make approximately 12 balls.
4. Place a lollipop stick into each ball. Cover hands well with vegetable shortening again and scrunch the balls in as tight as you can around the lollipop stick.
5. Leave on parchment-lined tray to set.

Hugs and Kisses

Makes 12

Take two of your favorite snacks, melt them together on a stick, and you end up with these totally delicious delights. In fact, you might have to make a double batch. Use any flavor of Hershey Kisses that strikes your fancy.

12 Hershey Kisses

24 square pretzels

1. Preheat oven to 350°F. Line a cookie sheet with parchment paper. Unwrap the kisses.
2. Place 12 pretzels on the parchment-lined cookie sheet. Top each pretzel with an unwrapped kiss.
3. Place cookie sheet into the oven for 1–2 minutes until the kisses start to look shiny.
4. Remove from oven. Working quickly and carefully, top with a lollipop stick and then press a pretzel down on top. Allow to cool and set.

USE ROLO CHOCOLATES IN PLACE OF HERSHEY KISSES.

Snickers Sticks

Chocolate, caramel, and peanuts—these treats have everything going for them. Could they get any better? Sure. Why not pop them on a stick, 'cause that makes everything cuter. Now they really have it all.

> 3 Snickers bars
> 6 tablespoons (3 ounces) unsalted butter
> 3 cups crispy rice cereal
> 1¼ cups (7 ounces) milk chocolate chips
> 2 tablespoons (1 ounce) unsalted butter
> ¼ milk chocolate chips extra

1. Line an 8" × 8" pan with aluminum foil and spray lightly with oil.
2. Chop the Snickers bars and pop into a large microwave-safe bowl with the 6 tablespoons butter. Microwave on medium for 30 seconds, remove from microwave, and stir carefully. Return to microwave and continue to heat in bursts of 30 seconds until the mixture is melted.
3. Stir in the crispy rice cereal and mix well. Spoon the mixture into the prepared pan and press down with your hands. Pop into the fridge until the mixture has set.
4. Melt the 1¼ cups milk chocolate chips in the microwave with 2 tablespoons of butter. Microwave on medium low for 60 seconds. Remove from microwave and stir. Return to microwave and continue to heat in bursts of 60 seconds at medium low until the mixture has melted. Spread the chocolate mixture onto the Snickers mixture in the pan. Return to the fridge to chill.
5. Once the mixture is set, turn out onto a cutting board. Using a knife, cut into 36 even slices.
6. Melt the remaining chocolate in the microwave on medium low heat. Dip the end of a lollipop stick into the chocolate and push it into the side of a Snickers slice. Repeat for all slices.

Chocolate Chip Cookie Truffle Pops

Makes 18

Follow these easy steps to take everyone's favorite cookie and turn it into a mouthwatering cake pop sensation. This is a great recipe to have on hand when you want to decorate pops quickly without all the fuss of baking a cake.

14-ounce package chocolate chip cookies
5 ounces cream cheese
14 ounces candy coating

1. Line a tray with parchment paper.
2. Crush chocolate chip cookies finely in a food processor. Add the cream cheese and process until the mixture comes together in clumps.
3. Take 4 teaspoons of mixture and roll into small balls and place on the parchment-lined tray. Using one of the pop sticks, make a hole in each cookie truffle and then pop the tray into fridge and chill until firm.
4. Melt the candy coating as described in the Melting Tips section in Chapter 2. Dip the end of each stick into the candy and push into the bottom of a cookie truffle. Return to parchment-lined tray and pop back into the fridge to chill for around 10 minutes.
5. Remelt the candy coating if necessary. Remove tray from fridge. Holding the end of the stick, dip a cookie truffle into the melted candy until the whole shape is submerged, and then lift it out of the melted candy. Holding the pop over the bowl to catch drips, gently tap the stick against your hand or the side of the bowl to remove excess candy coating. Once you have removed the excess candy, place the pops upright into a Styrofoam block to set.

Makes 16

Chocolate and rainbow chocolate chips combine to make a double dose of deliciousness in these crispy rice treats on a stick.

6 ounces chocolate chips
1 tablespoon (2 ounces) unsalted butter
¼ cup corn syrup
¼ cup powdered sugar
3 cups crispy rice cereal
¼ cup rainbow chip sprinkles
16 wooden paddle pop type sticks

1. Grease and line an 8" × 8" baking pan.
2. Place chocolate, butter, and corn syrup into a large microwave-safe bowl and heat in the microwave at medium low in 90-second bursts, stirring mixture in between each burst until all the chocolate is melted.
3. Add the sugar and crispy rice cereal and mix well with a spoon.
4. Spoon the mixture into the prepared pan. Sprinkle the rainbow chip sprinkles evenly over the top of the mixture and then press down with your hand to even the top. Place in the refrigerator to chill until set.
5. Once chilled, turn out onto a cutting board, cut into slices, and insert a wooden stick.

Super
Dooper
Double
Chocolate
Crispies

Crispy Nutter Pops

Makes around 16

Mix up these simple ingredients and the result is kind of like a breakfast pop on the go. Make sure you keep these chilled, as they become less stable on the sticks as they warm up.

- ¼ cup peanut butter
- ⅓ cup honey
- 2 cups crispy rice cereal
- 2 tablespoon confetti sprinkles

1. Line a cookie sheet with parchment paper.
2. Put peanut butter and honey in a medium-size bowl; mix and microwave for 30 seconds on medium. If the peanut butter is not melted, repeat for another 20 seconds. Mix well.
3. Mix the crispy rice cereal into the peanut butter and honey mixture; stir to combine. Fold in the sprinkles.
4. Using a couple of spoons (the dough will be sticky), drop 2 tablespoons of mixture onto the parchment-lined cookie sheet. Repeat until all mixture has been used. Pop in the fridge for an hour.
5. When the mixture has chilled, remove from fridge and use your fingers to shape the mixture into tight mounds.
6. Insert a lollipop stick into the top of each mound, ensuring you press the mixture in around the stick so it is secure. Place in refrigerator to set. When ready to serve, peel off paper carefully and transfer to a plate.

POP TIP

FOR A HEALTHIER OPTION, TRY USING NATURAL PEANUT BUTTER AND BROWN RICE CEREAL.

Crispy Nutter Pops

Tickle Sticks

Makes 24

Giggly girls and boys will be chasing each other around the yard and having too much fun to remember to eat.

10 ounces pink or light blue candy coating
24 long pretzel sticks
Sprinkles or sanding sugar

1. Line a tray with parchment paper.
2. Melt the candy coating as described in the Melting Tips section in Chapter 2. Dip the end of a pretzel into the coating, submerging it about 2", and then lift it out of the melted candy. Holding the pretzel over the bowl to catch drips, gently tap it against your hand or the side of the bowl to remove excess candy coating.
3. Move away from the bowl, still holding the end of the pretzel. Working quickly, shake the sprinkles over the candy coating before it has a chance to set. Place the pretzel onto the parchment-lined tray to set.
4. Repeat for remaining pretzels and then pop into the fridge to set for 10 minutes.

Dunk Me Donut Hole Pops

Makes 18

Do you have a weakness for delicious donuts? You'll be in donut-dunking heaven after trying these dippers. If you like, you can just use store-bought chocolate sauce warmed in the microwave and enjoy your dunkers even faster.

12 ounces chocolate candy coating
18 donut holes
Chocolate Dipping Sauce (see Chapter 9)

1. Line a tray with parchment paper.
2. Melt the candy coating in the microwave. Dip the end of the each lollipop stick into the melted candy and insert one into the bottom of each donut hole. Place on parchment-lined tray.
3. Using a spoon, drizzle a little extra melted chocolate candy coating over the top of the donut holes and leave to set.
4. Serve chocolate candy-drizzled donuts with warm Chocolate Dipping Sauce for dipping.

FOR A VARIATION, USE WHITE CANDY MELTS TO SECURE THE STICKS AND FOR THE DRIZZLE, AND BUY A GOOD QUALITY CARAMEL SAUCE TO DIP THE DONUTS IN.

Makes 16

Kids adore making their own ice-cream pops. Use vanilla or your favorite flavor. You can even use sorbet. Make sure you have a bit of space in your freezer for this recipe.

1 pint vanilla ice cream, softened in the fridge for 1 hour
18 ounces chocolate candy melts
4 tablespoons vegetable oil
3 tablespoons confetti sprinkles

1. Line a tray with parchment paper.
2. Scoop ice cream into balls using a 3 tablespoon-size ice-cream scooper. Place onto parchment-lined tray and pop into the freezer for an hour to freeze solid.
3. Place the candy melts and vegetable oil in a microwave-safe bowl. Heat on medium low at short bursts of 60 seconds, stirring between each burst, until the mixture is completely melted.
4. Dip the end of a lollipop stick into the melted candy and insert into an ice-cream ball. Return to the freezer to set for around 10 minutes.
5. Prepare a new tray lined with parchment paper.
6. Ensure that the melted chocolate is still smooth. If it isn't, return it to the microwave for 30 seconds or so, and stir well.
7. Holding the end of the lollipop stick, dip an ice-cream ball into the melted candy until submerged, and then lift it out of the melted candy. Holding the pop over the bowl to catch drips, gently tap the stick against your hand or the side of the bowl to remove excess candy coating. Place on the parchment-lined tray with the chocolate-covered ice-cream ball resting on the parchment paper. Lightly cover with the confetti sprinkles. Repeat with remaining ice-cream balls and return to freezer for an hour before serving.

POP TIP

SPRINKLE NUTS ON THE MELTED
CHOCOLATE IN THE LAST STEP
INSTEAD OF SPRINKLES.

Brownie Blast Pops

Brownie Blast Pops

Makes 16

Have a blast making and eating these super chocolaty treats. For some extra fun, try cutting the brownies into stars or other shapes using deep metal cookie cutters.

> 1 cup self-rising flour
> ⅓ cup cocoa
> 2½ tablespoons (5 ounces) unsalted butter
> 5 ounces semisweet chocolate
> 1¼ cups brown sugar, lightly packed
> 3 eggs
> 14 ounces chocolate candy coating
> 16 wooden paddle pop sticks
> Sprinkles any type

1. Preheat oven to 350°F. Grease and flour an 8" × 8" square baking pan and line bottom and sides with parchment paper.
2. Sift together the flour and cocoa. Set aside.
3. In a large bowl, melt the butter and chocolate in the microwave on medium-low heat for bursts of 90 seconds, stirring in between each burst until all the mixture is melted and lump free. Allow to cool a little.
4. Add the brown sugar and mix in with a whisk. Add all the eggs and whisk until combined.
5. Add the flour and cocoa mixture and stir with a spoon until just combined.
6. Pour into prepared pan and bake for 30 minutes.
7. Allow to cool in pan for 5 minutes and then turn out onto a wire rack to cool. Once cool, cut into 16 pieces.
8. Line a tray with parchment paper.
9. Melt the candy coating as described in the Melting Tips section in Chapter 2.
10. Dip the end of one of the wooden sticks into the melted candy. Push into a brownie and place onto the parchment tray. Repeat for remaining brownies and then pop the tray into the fridge to chill for 30 minutes.
11. Remelt the candy coating and remove the tray from the fridge.
12. Holding the end of the wooden stick, dip a whole brownie into the melted candy until it's submerged. Allow excess candy coating to drip off and then place the brownie on the parchment-lined tray. Gently cover with sprinkles. Repeat for remaining brownies.
13. Store in an airtight container for up to 3 days.

Raspberry and Cream Clouds

Makes 13

Meringue joined with fruity cream adds up to a dreamy light-as-air confection. White chocolate can melt very easily in hot weather, so halve the cream in the recipe if you are expecting a hot day. The baked meringues can be kept in an airtight container for 2 days, but once the treat is assembled, it is best eaten within a few hours.

2 egg whites

½ cup sugar

¼ teaspoon cream of tartar

½ teaspoon vanilla extract

2 tablespoons heavy cream

4 ounces white chocolate

12 raspberries, mashed (frozen or fresh)

1. **To make the meringues:** Preheat oven to 250°F. Line 2 cookie sheets with parchment paper.
2. Whip egg whites in a large bowl until soft peaks form. Mix in the sugar, a tablespoon at a time, allowing the mixture to combine well after each addition. Add the cream of tartar and vanilla and beat until all ingredients are dissolved and well mixed. The mixture should be stiff.
3. Spoon mounds of the mixture, around 2 teaspoons each, onto the prepared cookie sheets, leaving ½" between mounds.
4. Bake for 1 hour. Without removing the cookie sheets, turn the oven off. Leave the meringues in the oven with the door closed for another 10 minutes. Remove from oven and allow to cool on the cookie sheets before removing from parchment paper.
5. **To make the raspberry cream:** In a medium-size microwave-safe dish, melt the cream and white chocolate at medium-low heat in bursts of 60 seconds until melted. Stir well between each burst. Add the raspberries; mix until combined. Leave to set until it is thick enough to spoon but not set hard.
6. Spoon 1 teaspoon of the mixture onto the flat side of one meringue, stick in a lollipop stick, and then press another meringue on top. Repeat until all the meringues are used. Place in an airtight container and pop into the fridge until the raspberry cream mixture has set.

POP TIP

FOR A DARK CHOCOLATE MINT VERSION, MELT 4 OUNCES DARK CHOCOLATE WITH 3 TABLESPOONS HEAVY CREAM IN THE MICROWAVE AT MEDIUM-LOW HEAT AND STIR IN ½ TEASPOON PEPPERMINT EXTRACT. ALLOW MIXTURE TO NEARLY SET AND THEN SPOON INTO MERINGUES AS IN THE LAST STEP FOR RASPBERRY CREAM.

Sprinkly Swirly Bread Stakes

Makes 12

Sure, it's not for every day, but this swirly, sugary bread makes an enticing treat for special occasions. These treats are best eaten the day they're made.

- 12 pieces white bread
- Butter or margarine
- ½ cup rainbow nonpareils, miniature confetti sprinkles, or rainbow chip sprinkles
- 12 skewers

1. Butter each slice of bread, sprinkle with the candy, and press down lightly with your fingers to make sure the candy will mostly stay stuck to the bread.
2. Cut the crusts off the bread and roll up one slice like a jellyroll. Cut the roll into 3 slices.
3. Push all 3 swirled slices onto a skewer.
4. Repeat for remaining bread, placing 3 swirls onto each skewer.

POP TIP

TRY USING NUTELLA INSTEAD OF BUTTER FOR A YUMMY CHOCOLATE SWIRL VERSION.

Sticky Cinnamon Roll Sticks

Makes 12

This is a cheater's version of cinnamon rolls, with no kneading dough and waiting around.

- ½ stick (2 ounces) unsalted butter, softened
- ⅔ cup sugar
- 2 teaspoons ground cinnamon
- 1 package frozen puff pastry dough sheets, thawed (2 sheets, around 17.3 ounces)
- 12 wooden paddle pop sticks
- 1 cup powdered sugar
- ⅓ cup milk or cream
- 1 tablespoon maple syrup

1. Preheat oven to 350°F. Line a cookie sheet with aluminum foil.
2. In a medium bowl mix together the butter, sugar, and cinnamon with a spoon until well combined.
3. Spread ½ of the cinnamon mixture evenly over one of the sheets and then roll it up, starting from the long side, to make a long log. Cut the log into 6 pieces and lay each piece onto the prepared cookie sheet. Repeat with the remaining sheet of puff pastry and cinnamon mixture. Gently push a wooden stick about halfway into each of the rolls.
4. Bake 25–30 minutes until golden. Leave to cool a little on the cookie sheets and then, using a spatula, lift them onto a wire rack to cool, being careful not to disturb the sticks.
5. Sift the powdered sugar into a bowl and mix in cream and maple syrup.
6. Top each roll with a dollop of the maple syrup glaze and serve.

Sweets
for my
Sweet

Sticky
Cinnamon
Roll Sticks

Bitty Maple Waffle Bites

Makes 12

Maple syrup and waffles combine to make a heavenly pop that's really hard to beat. Serve with Chocolate Dipping Sauce (Chapter 9) for a truly decadent experience.

12 waffles

2 cups powdered sugar

¼ cup heavy cream

2 tablespoons maple syrup

1. Cut each waffle in half.
2. Cover a tray with parchment paper and lay 12 waffle halves on the tray.
3. Sift the sugar into a medium-size bowl, add the cream and maple syrup, and mix with a spoon until smooth.
4. Spoon 2 teaspoons of maple filling onto each waffle half on the tray. Press a lollipop stick into the maple filling on each half and then top with a plain waffle half, pressing down gently.
5. Allow to set for an hour or until the sticks are secure.

Absolutely Scrumptious!

Bitty Maple Waffle Bites

YUM!!!

Makes 36

Serve up a favorite winter warmer with flair when you bring out these beauties. Hot chocolate sticks make a nifty gift to a teacher or someone else special when packaged in a pretty box by themselves or with a mug. Plus, as a super bonus, they taste like delicious chocolate fudge when eaten straight from the stick.

½ cup heavy cream

10 ounces sweetened condensed milk

2 11.5 ounce bags semisweet chocolate chips

Mini marshmallows

1. Line an 8" × 8" pan with aluminum foil.
2. In a large microwave-safe bowl, heat the cream and condensed milk on high for 60 seconds.
3. Mix in the chocolate and stir. Allow chocolate to melt for a minute, and stir again. If the chocolate has not all melted, return to microwave at medium heat for 60 seconds. Remove and stir. Repeat if required.
4. Use a spoon or whisk to mix until the mixture is thick and shiny.
5. Pour chocolate mixture into the prepared pan and sprinkle with the mini marshmallows. Press down the marshmallows gently and allow the pan to set overnight at room temperature.
6. Once set, turn out onto a clean cutting surface and carefully remove the foil. Slice into 1¼" cubes (or size desired for serving), using a knife that has been heated in hot water and wiped dry before each cut. Stick a wooden stick into the center of each block. Store in an airtight container in the fridge for up to 10 days.
7. To use, heat 1 cup of milk for each square, pour into a mug, and stir the hot chocolate stick into the milk until melted. Assist small children with this, and allow the milk to cool a bit before they attempt to drink it.

Hot Chocolate on a Stick

Dressed-Up Oreo Cookies

Makes 12

Dress up everyday Oreo cookies with a chocolate coating and sprinkles that make the cookies not only look great but taste super fantastic.

1 package Oreo cookies

14 ounces candy coating

Sprinkles any kind

1. Line two trays with parchment paper.
2. Twist the top off each cookie and lay it on the parchment paper next to its matching cookie half.
3. Using a lollipop stick, push an indent into each cream-topped cookie half about ¾" into the cream. Repeat for all cookies.
4. Melt the candy coating as described in the Melting Tips section in Chapter 2. Dip the end of a lollipop stick into the melted chocolate. Put the candy-dipped lollipop stick into the indent you have made on a cream-topped cookie half. Using a spoon, scoop up about ¼ teaspoon extra melted candy coating and place it over the top of the lollipop stick. Pick up the top half of the cookie and gently press it back onto the matching bottom until you feel it is secure.
5. Repeat for remaining cookies and pop into the fridge for 15 minutes to set.
6. Remelt the candy coating. Remove tray from fridge. Holding the end of the lollipop stick, dip a whole Oreo cookie until it is submerged in the candy coating, and then lift it out of the melted candy. Holding the pop over the bowl to catch drips, gently tap the stick against your hand or the side of the bowl to remove excess candy coating. Once you have removed the excess candy, place the pop onto the parchment paper to set and quickly shake some of the sprinkles over it.
7. Repeat for remaining cookies.

Festive Oreo Cookies

Makes 12

Pop these into a pretty pail or jar filled with peppermint candy to a make an enchanting centerpiece for a Christmas celebration.

12 Oreo cookies

14 ounces white candy coating

12 mini candy canes

1. Line two trays with parchment paper.
2. Twist the top off each cookie and lay it on the parchment paper next to its matching cookie half.
3. Using a lollipop stick, push an indent into each cream-topped cookie half about ¾" into the cream. Repeat for all cookies.
4. Melt the candy coating as described in the Melting Tips section in Chapter 2. Dip the end of a lollipop stick into

the melted chocolate. Put the candy-dipped lollipop stick into the indent you have made on a cream-topped cookie half. Using a spoon, scoop up about ¼ teaspoon extra melted candy coating and place it over the top of the lollipop stick. Pick up the top half of the cookie and gently press it back onto the matching bottom until you feel it is secure.

5. Repeat for remaining cookies and pop into the fridge for 10 minutes to set.

6. Remelt the candy coating. Remove tray from fridge. Holding the end of the lollipop stick, dip a whole Oreo cookie until it is submerged in the candy coating, and then lift it out of the melted candy. Holding the pop over the bowl to catch drips, gently tap the stick against your hand or the side of the bowl to remove excess candy coating. Once you have removed the excess candy, place the pop onto the parchment paper to set and quickly place a candy cane on top of the dipped cookie before the candy coating has a chance to set.

7. Repeat for remaining cookies.

IF YOU CAN'T FIND MINI CANES, BUY SOME LARGER ONES, CRUSH THEM, AND SPRINKLE ONTO THE DIPPED COOKIES BEFORE THE CANDY COATING SETS.

Makes 25 pops

Could it even be possible to make Oreo cookies better? Yes it is, but be careful—these delicious morsels are totally addictive.

1 18-ounce package Oreo cookies
1 8-ounce package cream cheese, cubed
14 ounces candy coating (any color)

1. Line a tray with parchment paper.

2. Crush Oreo cookies finely in a food processor. Add the cream cheese cubes and process until the mixture comes together in clumps.

3. Take 4 teaspoons of mixture and roll into small balls and place on parchment-lined tray. Using one of the pop sticks, make a hole in each cookie truffle, and then pop the tray into the fridge. Chill until firm.

4. Melt the candy coating as described in the Melting Tips section in Chapter 2. Dip the end of each stick into the candy and push into the bottom of a cookie truffle. Return to parchment-lined tray and pop back into the fridge to chill for around 10 minutes.

5. Remelt the candy coating if necessary. Remove tray from fridge. Holding the end of the stick, dip a cookie truffle into the melted candy until the whole shape is submerged, and then lift it out of the melted candy. Holding the pop over the bowl to catch drips, gently tap the stick against your hand or the side of the bowl to remove excess candy coating. Once you have removed the excess candy coating, place each pop upright into a Styrofoam block to set.

S'more Dipped Pops

Makes 12

This campfire classic is even better on a stick. Just as tasty, just less of a mess—on your hands at least. Switch up the s'more a little by putting the chocolate on the outside instead of inside.

6 whole graham crackers (24 squares)

12 marshmallows

12 lollipop sticks

7 ounces chocolate candy coating

1. Preheat oven to 350°F. Line a cookie sheet with parchment paper.
2. Break each graham cracker down the center to make 2 even pieces. Place 12 pieces on the baking tray and reserve the other 12 for later in the recipe.
3. Top each cracker with a marshmallow. Place into the oven for 5–10 minutes until the marshmallow starts to melt but before it turns golden.
4. Remove from the oven and lay a lollipop stick on top of each marshmallow. Top with one of the reserved graham crackers and press down to secure. Repeat for remaining s'mores. Allow to cool on cookie sheets.
5. Melt the candy coating in the microwave at medium-low heat for 60 seconds and then stir. Continue heating in this manner for 60-second bursts until the candy coating is melted. Pick up a s'more pop by the end of the lollipop stick and dip it halfway into the candy coating. Lift it out of the melted candy, continuing to hold the pop upside down over the bowl. Allow excess candy coating to drip off the pop and then lay the pop back down on the baking tray until chocolate has set.

Ice-Cream Cookie Sandwich

Makes 12

Buy your favorite chocolate chip cookies from the grocery store or make your own—it doesn't really matter. The key here is to get that yummy cookie goodness wrapped around the creamy ice cream.

24 chocolate chip cookies (store-bought or make Full of Chocolate Chips Cookies from Chapter 4 without the lollipop sticks)

1 pint ice cream, slightly softened

12 wooden paddle pop sticks

1. Line a tray with parchment paper.
2. Place 12 of the chocolate chip cookies on the parchment-lined tray with the flat side facing upward.
3. Scoop around 2 tablespoons of ice cream on top of each cookie, insert the wooden stick into the side of the ice cream so it is laying parallel with the tray and then press another cookie, flat side down, on top. Repeat for remaining cookies and then pop the tray into the fridge to chill for 1 hour.
4. If not serving immediately, wrap each cookie sandwich in aluminum foil and store in an airtight container in the freezer for up to 1 month.

POP TIP

FOR AN EXTRA DECADENT TREAT, TAKE AROUND 10 OUNCES OF CHOCOLATE CANDY COATING, MELT USING THE INSTRUCTIONS IN CHAPTER 2, AND DIP THE ICE CREAM SANDWICHES HALFWAY INTO THE MELTED CHOCOLATE.

Makes 12

These charming Christmas treats are deceptively simple and fabulous to eat. They make great Christmas dinner sweets and an ideal teacher's gift when packaged in a pretty box.

30 red jelly beans

14 ounces green candy coating

2 cups shredded coconut

1. Line 2 trays with parchment paper.
2. Using safety scissors, cut each jelly bean in half.
3. Melt the candy coating in a microwave-safe bowl at medium-low heat in short bursts of 60 seconds each, for a total of about 4–6 minutes. Stir in between each burst.
4. Remove from microwave and stir in the shredded coconut until well combined.
5. Working quickly, before the melted candy has time to set, drop about 4 teaspoons of mixture onto the parchment paper and shape it into a ring with a hole at the center, like a wreath. Insert a lollipop stick into the bottom of the ring/wreath and then press 5 halves of the jelly beans into the circle. Repeat for remaining mixture. If the mixtures starts to set before all the wreaths are made, return it to the microwave for 60 seconds at medium low.
6. Leave to set on the parchment-lined tray. Store in an airtight container for up to a week.

Coconut
Christmas
Wreaths

Merry Christmas

Mint Patties

These fresh minty sweets require no stovetop or oven baking and only a few ingredients, which make them great for kids to mix up. Small children may need some help to get the mixture combined without a bit of fun mess, so be prepared with aprons and paper towels.

2¼ cups powdered sugar

1½ teaspoons corn syrup

1½ teaspoons water

½ teaspoon peppermint extract

1 tablespoon Crisco (or other vegetable shortening)

1" round cutter

18 ounces red candy coating

20 lollipops sticks

1. Line a tray with parchment paper.
2. In a medium bowl mix the sugar, corn syrup, water, peppermint extract, and Crisco at medium speed until well combined. Alternatively mix by hand with a large spoon.
3. Dust work surface with sifted powdered sugar and lightly knead the sugar-peppermint mixture until smooth.
4. Dust the work surface again and using a large rolling pin roll out the mixture until ½" thick. Cut out round shapes using the 1" cutter dusted with a little powdered sugar. Knead together any leftover mixture, roll out, and cut out more round shapes; repeat until all the mixture is used. Place the mint rounds on the parchment-lined tray.
5. Melt the candy coating as described in the Melting Tips section in Chapter 2. Dip the end of a lollipop stick into the melted candy and then insert into the side of a round so that the stick is parallel with the tray, pushing the stick in about ½". Repeat for remaining mixture and place in fridge to firm for about 15 minutes.
6. Remelt the candy coating if necessary. Remove tray from fridge. Holding the end of the stick, dip a mint round into the melted candy until the whole shape is submerged, and then lift it out of the melted candy. Holding the pop over the bowl to catch drips, gently tap the stick against your hand or the side of the bowl to remove excess candy coating. Remove as much excess as possible before you put the pop into the Styrofoam block to set. Repeat with remaining mint rounds.

CHAPTER 6
Cutie Pie Pops

Have everyone squealing with delight with these too-cute-for-words pies on a stick. You can either make your own pie crust using the recipes in this chapter or buy premade pie dough from the supermarket. Carefully follow the instructions for the amount of filling to be placed in each pie pop. If you use any more than what's called for, your pies will overflow during the baking process.

Sugar Crust Pie Dough

Makes 9 pie pops

A recipe that's easy to roll and reroll, which is great when the kids are helping out—no need to worry about redo's. You can mix this dough either by hand or in a food processor, making the preparation even easier.

2 cups all-purpose flour
½ cup granulated sugar
½ teaspoon baking soda
¼ teaspoon salt
1 stick (4 ounces) butter, chilled and cut into small cubes
1 egg

1. Sift flour, sugar, baking soda, and salt together. Using your fingertips, rub in the butter quickly and then mix in egg to form a firm dough. (To prepare in a food processor, put the sifted flour mixture into the processor and add the butter, pulsing until the butter is evenly distributed. Add egg and pulse until mixture clumps together to form a dough.) Wrap in plastic wrap and chill in fridge for 10 to 30 minutes.
2. When ready to use the dough, pull off a small section and knead. Because you are making small shapes, you can roll out just a small section at a time.
3. Before rolling out the pie dough, dust the work surface with a little sifted flour. Roll out the dough to ¼" thickness. Lift the dough, turn it, and dust with more flour underneath if required to keep it from sticking.

Chocolate Pie Dough

Makes 9 pie pops

If you think that chocolate goes with everything, you can use this chocolate dough in place of the Sugar Crust Pie Dough for a chocolaty change with any of the pie recipes.

1½ cups all-purpose flour
⅓ cup unsweetened cocoa powder
½ cup sugar
6 tablespoons (3 ounces) unsalted butter, cut into cubes
¼ teaspoon salt
2–3 tablespoons cold water
1 egg yolk

1. Place flour, cocoa, sugar, butter, and salt into food processor and pulse until well mixed. Add 2 tablespoons of water and the whole egg yolk and pulse. If the mixture does not come together, continue to add water 1 teaspoon at a time until the mixture forms a dense dough. To make without a processor sift flour, cocoa, sugar, and salt together. Using your fingertips, rub in the butter quickly. Mix in 2 tablespoons of water and quickly knead to form a firm dough; add up to 1 tablespoon extra water if required if dough is too dry.
2. Wrap in plastic wrap and chill in fridge for 10–30 minutes. When you are ready to make the pops, remove dough from fridge and pull off a handful. Knead it a little so that it will be easier to roll out.
3. Before rolling out the pie dough, dust the work surface with a little sifted flour. Roll out the dough to ¼" thickness. Lift the dough, turn it, and dust with more flour underneath if required to keep it from sticking.

Berry Good Fruit Jam Pie Pops

Makes 9 pie pops

Simply delicious! The key to this pie's appeal is using a good-quality, tasty fruit jam. Let the kids pick their favorite flavor and it's sure to be a winner.

1 batch Sugar Crust Pie Dough
½ cup berry jam
Small amount milk and pastry brush

1. Line 2 cookie sheets with parchment paper.
2. Cut out a 2½" round of pastry and place onto the parchment-lined cookie sheet. Lightly press about 1" of the end of a lollipop stick into the round of pie dough.
3. Spread 1 rounded teaspoon jam in the center of each round, leaving about ½" around the edge.
4. Cut out another 2½" round to top the pie. If you like, you can cut out a decorative shape from the center of this round. Place on top of the jam-covered round and gently press together the edges.
5. Using a lollipop stick or the ends of a fork, firmly press the edges together in a decorative pattern. Repeat process until all the pie dough is used.
6. Pop the unbaked pies into the fridge while you heat the oven to 350°F.
7. Once the oven is heated, use a pastry brush to brush each pie with a small amount of milk. Pop the pies in the oven.
8. Bake about 15 minutes, until golden brown. Remove from oven and allow to cool on cookie sheets.

Berry Good Fruit Jam Pie Pops

Cherry Love Pie Pops

Makes 9 pie pops

You'll fall in love with these pretty pies once you have tried them. The recipe suggests using a heart-shape cutter, which is very cute, but the pie will taste just as delicious if you use a round cutter.

1 batch Sugar Crust Pie Dough
½ cup cherry pie filling, each cherry cut in half
Small amount milk and pastry brush

1. Line 2 cookie sheets with parchment paper.
2. Cut out a 2½" heart shape of pastry and place onto the parchment-lined cookie sheet. Lightly press about 1" of the end of a lollipop stick onto the pointed bottom section of the pie dough heart.
3. Place 4 cherry halves and a bit of the pie liquid in the center of each heart, leaving about ½" around the edge.
4. Cut out another 2½" heart from the pie dough. If you like, you can cut out a decorative shape from the center of this heart. Place over the top of the cherry-covered heart and gently press together the edges.
5. Using a lollipop stick or the ends of a fork, firmly press the edges together in a decorative pattern. Repeat until all the pie dough is used.
6. Pop the unbaked pies into the fridge while you heat the oven to 350°F.
7. Once the oven is heated, use a pastry brush to brush each pie with a small amount of milk. Pop the pies in the oven.
8. Bake about 16 minutes, until golden brown. Remove from oven and allow to cool on cookie sheets.

Cherry Love Pie Pops

Peanut Butter and Jelly Pie Pops

The classic union of peanut butter and jelly makes for an innovative pie pop. Use either crunchy or smooth peanut butter, whichever you prefer. If you're feeling a bit decadent, sneak in a couple of chocolate chips before baking.

1 batch Sugar Crust Pie Dough
¼ cup peanut butter
2 teaspoons dark corn syrup
2 tablespoons sugar
1 teaspoon vanilla
½ cup jelly
Small amount milk and a pastry brush

1. Line 2 cookie sheets with parchment paper.
2. In a small bowl mix together the peanut butter, corn syrup, sugar, and vanilla.
3. Cut out a 2½" round of pastry and place onto the parchment-lined cookie sheet. Lightly press about 1" of the end of a lollipop stick into the round of pie dough.
4. Spread ¾ teaspoon jelly in the center of each round, leaving about ½" around the edge. Then dollop ¾ teaspoon peanut butter mixture onto the top of each jam-covered pie round.
5. Cut out another 2½" round to top the pie. If you like, you can cut out a decorative shape from the center of this round. Place on top of the jam-covered round and gently press together the edges.
6. Using a lollipop stick or the ends of a fork, firmly press the edges together in a decorative pattern. Repeat process until all the pie dough is used.
7. Pop the unbaked pies into the fridge while you heat the oven to 350°F.
8. Once the oven is heated, use a pastry brush to brush each pie with a small amount of milk. Pop the pies in the oven.
9. Bake about 15 minutes, until golden brown. Remove from oven and allow to cool on cookie sheets.

Lemon Curd Pie Pops

Makes 9 pie pops

Tangy lemon curd merges with a dollop of cream cheese to make a pie a touch reminiscent of a cheesecake.

1 batch Sugar Crust Pie Dough
½ cup lemon curd
2 ounces cream cheese at room temperature
Small amount milk and pastry brush
Granulated sugar for sprinkling

1. Line 2 cookie sheets with parchment paper.
2. Cut out a 2½" round of pastry and place onto the parchment-lined cookie sheet. Lightly press about 1" of the end of a lollipop stick into the round of pie dough.
3. Spread 1 rounded teaspoon lemon curd in the center of each round, leaving about ½" around the edge. Place ½ teaspoon of cream cheese on top of the lemon curd.
4. Cut out another 2½" round to top the pie. If you like, you can cut out a decorative shape from the center of this round. Place on top of the curd-covered round and gently press together the edges.
5. Using a lollipop stick or the ends of a fork, firmly press the edges together in a decorative pattern. Repeat process until all the pie dough is used.
6. Pop the unbaked pies into the fridge while you heat the oven to 350°F.
7. Once the oven is heated, use a pastry brush to brush each pie with a small amount of milk. Sprinkle a little sugar over the top of each pie.
8. Bake about 15 minutes, until golden brown. Remove from oven and allow to cool on cookie sheets.

Pecan Pie Pops

Makes 9 pie pops

This simple buttery sugar crust surrounding pecans coated in caramel syrup is a sure-fire recipe for yumminess.

1 batch Sugar Crust Pie Dough
¼ cup dark corn syrup
1 tablespoon dark brown sugar
2 tablespoons (1 ounce) softened unsalted butter
1 egg, lightly beaten
½ cup chopped pecans
Small amount milk and pastry brush

1. Line 2 cookie sheets with parchment paper.
2. In a bowl mix together corn syrup, sugar, and butter until well combined. Add the egg and mix until combined. Stir in the pecans.
3. Cut out a 2½" round of pastry and place onto the parchment-lined cookie sheet. Lightly press about 1" of the end of a lollipop stick into the round of pie dough.
4. Spoon 1 rounded teaspoon pecan mixture in the center of each round, leaving about ½" around the edge.
5. Cut out another 2½" round to top the pie. Place over the top of the pecan-covered round and gently press together the edges.
6. Using a lollipop stick or the ends of a fork, firmly press the edges together in a decorative pattern. Repeat the process until all the pie dough is used.
7. Pop the unbaked pies into the fridge while you heat the oven to 350°F.
8. Once the oven is heated, use a pastry brush to brush each pie with a small amount of milk. Pop the pies in the oven.
9. Bake about 15 minutes, until golden brown. Remove from oven and allow to cool on cookie sheets.

Apple Cinnamon Pie Pops

Makes 9 pie pops

Classic apple and cinnamon pie meets contemporary pop. If you prefer, use your favorite premade apple pie filling instead of making your own.

- 1 batch Sugar Crust Pie Dough
- 1 large apple
- ½ teaspoon lemon juice
- 1 teaspoon water
- 1 teaspoon all-purpose flour
- 1 teaspoon sugar
- ½ teaspoon cinnamon
- 1 tablespoon sugar (optional; for top of pies)
- ¼ teaspoon cinnamon (optional; for top of pies)
- Small amount milk and pastry brush

1. Preheat oven to 350°F. Line 2 cookie sheets with parchment paper.
2. Peel, core, and cut the apple into small pieces; it should make around 1 cup. Place in a medium-size microwave-safe bowl with lemon juice and water, mix together, and microwave on high for 60 seconds. Remove from microwave and stir. Repeat this process two more times, for a total cooking time of 3 minutes. Remove from microwave and cover until cool.
3. When apple mixture is cool, mix in flour, 1 teaspoon sugar, and ½ teaspoon cinnamon. In a separate bowl, make topping by combining 1 tablespoon sugar and ¼ teaspoon cinnamon.
4. Cut out a 2½" round of pastry and place onto the parchment-lined cookie sheet. Lightly press about 1" of the end of a lollipop stick into the round of pie dough.
5. Spoon about 1½ teaspoons apple mixture in the center of each round, leaving about ½" around the edge.
6. Cut out another 2½" round to top the pie. If you like, you can cut out a decorative shape from the center of this round. Place on top of the apple-covered round and gently press together the edges.
7. Using a lollipop stick or the ends of a fork, firmly press the edges together in a decorative pattern. Repeat process until all the pie dough is used.
8. Use a pastry brush to brush each pie with a small amount of milk. If you like, sprinkle the combined cinnamon sugar over the top.
9. Bake about 15 minutes, until golden brown. Remove from oven and allow to cool on cookie sheets.

FOR SOMETHING A LITTLE BIT DIFFERENT, SPRINKLE A LITTLE BIT OF SHREDDED CHEDDAR CHEESE ON THE TOP OF THE PIES IN PLACE OF THE CINNAMON SUGAR.

Boston
Cream Pie
Pops

Makes 12 pies

Take this creamy dreamy pie to new heights, and then put it up high on a pedestal just as it deserves.

- 1 batch vanilla cupcakes (see Chapter 3, use the recipe for Quick and Easy Mini Vanilla Cupcakes and bake for 20–25 minutes without paper baking cups in regular-sized muffin tins that have been greased)
- 1 cup heavy cream
- 1½ tablespoons cornstarch
- 2 tablespoons sugar
- 1 large egg yolk
- 1 teaspoon vanilla extract
- 1 cup (6 ounces) semisweet chocolate chips
- ⅔ cup heavy cream
- 12 Pastry Pedestals

1. **To make pastry cream:** In a large microwave-safe bowl, whisk together 1 cup cream, cornstarch, and sugar. Place in microwave and cook at high for 60 seconds. Remove from microwave and stir the mixture. Repeat two or three times more, cooking 60 seconds at a time, until the mixture starts to boil and thickens slightly. Be very careful of the hot bowl.

2. While you are cooking the cream mixture in the microwave, whisk together the egg yolk and vanilla in a small bowl.

3. Carefully whisk a couple of tablespoons of the hot cream mixture into the egg yolk a teaspoon at a time. Ensure the mixture is mixed in well before the next addition; if you add too much at a time, the yolk may cook too quickly and become lumpy. Pour the egg yolk mixture back into the large bowl and mix all the ingredients together well. Return to the microwave and cook on high for 30 seconds. Remove and stir. The mixture should be thick; if the mixture is not, return and cook another 10 seconds at high.

4. Pour the mixture into another bowl. Do not stir at this stage. Press down some plastic wrap onto the surface of the cream mixture to prevent a skin from forming. Allow to cool to room temperature.

5. **To make chocolate glaze:** Place the chocolate chips and ⅔ cup cream in a microwave-safe bowl and heat at medium low in bursts of 30 seconds. Stir between each burst until the mixture is melted and smooth.

6. To assemble pies, split the cupcakes in half and spoon about 1 tablespoon of the pastry cream on the bottom half of each cupcake. Place the top half of each cupcake on top of the pastry cream. Spread about 1 tablespoon of the chocolate glaze on the top of each cupcake. Place in fridge for 30 minutes to chill.

7. Follow manufacturer's instructions to assemble the Pastry Pedestals. Insert the pedestals into a Styrofoam block to hold them upright.

8. When the pies are chilled, remove from the fridge and place the finished Boston Cream Pie Pops on Pastry Pedestal.

Blueberry Pie Pops

Makes 9 pie pops

Sweet and juicy blueberries make a great filling for these summertime pie pops. Serve with a small dish of whipped cream for dipping.

1 batch Sugar Crust Pie Dough

1 cup blueberries (if using frozen, defrost)

Squeeze of lemon juice

1 teaspoon all-purpose flour

1 teaspoon sugar

¼ teaspoon cinnamon

Small amount milk and pastry brush

1. Preheat oven to 350°F.
2. In a bowl mix together blueberries, lemon juice, flour, sugar, and cinnamon.
3. Cut out a 2½" round of pastry and place onto the parchment-lined cookie sheet. Lightly press about 1" of the end of a lollipop stick into the round of pie dough.
4. Spoon about 6 blueberries in the center of each round, leaving about ½" around the edge.
5. Cut out another 2½" round to top the pie. If you like, you can cut out a decorative shape from the center of this round. Place on top of the blueberry-covered round and gently press together the edges.
6. Using a lollipop stick or the ends of a fork, firmly press the edges together in a decorative pattern. Repeat process until all the pie dough is used.
7. Pop the unbaked pies into the fridge while you heat the oven to 350°F.
8. Once the oven is heated, use a pastry brush to brush each pie with a small amount of milk. Pop the pies in the oven.
9. Bake about 15 minutes, until golden brown. Remove from oven and allow to cool on cookie sheets.

Triple Chocolate Fudge Pie Pops

No need for the kids to make mud pies anymore once they get the hang of this pie. It's three layers of chocolate!

1 batch Chocolate Pie Dough
½ cup chocolate chips (about 4 ounces)
4 tablespoons (2 ounces) unsalted butter
Small amount milk and pastry brush
7 ounces chocolate candy coating

1. Preheat oven to 350°F.
2. Melt chocolate and butter in the microwave on medium-low heat for 60 seconds. Remove from microwave and stir. Return to microwave and repeat until the chocolate is melted (2–3 minutes total).
3. Cut out a 2½" round of pastry and place onto a parchment-lined cookie sheet. Lightly press about 1" of the end of a lollipop stick into the round of pie dough.
4. Spoon 1 rounded teaspoon chocolate mixture in the center of each round, leaving about ½" around the edge. Lightly brush milk around the edge of the round.
5. Cut out another 2½" round to top the pie. If you like, you can cut out a decorative shape from the center of this round. Place on top of the chocolate-covered round and gently press together the edges.
6. Using a lollipop stick or the ends of a fork, firmly press the edges together in a decorative pattern. Repeat process until all the pie dough is used.
7. Bake about 15 minutes or until you can see the pie dough is cooked all the way to the middle. Remove from oven and allow to cool on cookie sheets.
8. Once the pies are cooled, melt the candy coating as described in the Melting Tips section in Chapter 2. Using a spoon, drizzle the candy coating over the pies generously.

Triple Chocolate Fudge Pie Pops

Sweet Strawberry Pie Pops

Makes 9 pie pops

Freshly picked succulent strawberries and vanilla baked in a buttery pie dough come together to make a scrumptious pie pop.

> **1 batch Sugar Crust Pie Dough**
> **1 cup strawberries, sliced**
> **Squeeze of lemon juice**
> **1 teaspoon all-purpose flour**
> **1 teaspoon sugar**
> **½ teaspoon vanilla extract**
> **Small amount milk and pastry brush**
> **Pink sanding sugar (optional)**

1. Preheat oven to 350°F. Line 2 cookie sheets with parchment paper.
2. In a bowl mix together strawberries, lemon juice, flour, sugar, and vanilla.
3. Cut out a 2½" round of pastry and place onto the parchment-lined cookie sheet. Lightly press about 1" of the end of a lollipop stick into the round of pie dough.
4. Spoon about 1 to 1½ teaspoons strawberry mixture in the center of each round, leaving about ½" around the edge.
5. Cut out another 2½" round to top the pie. If you like, you can cut out a decorative shape from the center of this round. Place on top of the strawberry-covered round and gently press together the edges.
6. Using a lollipop stick or the ends of a fork, firmly press the edges together in a decorative pattern. Repeat process until all the pie dough is used.
7. Use a pastry brush to brush each pie with a small amount of milk. If you like, sprinkle a little pink sanding sugar over the top.
8. Bake about 12–15 minutes, until golden brown. Remove from oven and allow to cool on cookie sheets.

Makes 9 pie pops

Perfectly sized for just one person, these pies could be just the thing to make sure you don't overindulge at Thanksgiving or just anytime. Or perhaps they might be so good you won't be able to stop at just one.

1 batch Sugar Crust Pie Dough
1 cup pumpkin pie filling (prespiced filling)
1 egg
Small amount milk and pastry brush
Cinnamon (optional)

1. Line 2 trays with parchment paper.
2. In a medium bowl mix together the pumpkin pie filling and egg until combined.
3. Cut out a 2½" round of pastry and place onto the parchment-lined cookie sheet. Lightly press about 1" of the end of a lollipop stick into the round of pie dough.
4. Spread 1½ teaspoon pumpkin mixture in the center of each round, leaving about ½" around the edge.
5. Cut out another 2½" round to top the pie. If you like, you can cut out a decorative shape from the center of this round. Place on top of the pumpkin-covered round and gently press together the edges.

6. Using a lollipop stick or the ends of a fork, firmly press the edges together in a decorative pattern. Repeat process until all the pie dough is used.
7. Pop the uncooked pies into the fridge while you heat the oven to 350°F.
8. Once the oven is heated, use a pastry brush to brush each pie with a small amount of milk. Sprinkle a little cinnamon over the top and pop the pies in the oven.
9. Bake about 15 minutes, until golden brown. Remove from oven and allow to cool on cookie sheets.

IF YOU PREFER, YOU CAN MAKE YOUR OWN PUMPKIN PIE FILLING BY COOKING AND PURÉEING 1 CUP OF FRESH PUMPKIN AND ADDING PUMPKIN PIE SPICE MIX TO TASTE. WHEN FINISHED, FOLLOW THE REST OF THE RECIPE AS IS.

Makes 9 pie pops

Shiver me timbers these pie pops be delicious, and the kids will think these treasures are so neat they'll be willing to walk the plank to try this recipe out.

> 1 batch Bluberry Pie Pops (or any flavor)
> ¼ batch Marshmallow Fondant (see Chapter 9) (¾ red and ¼ black)
> 1 batch Royal Icing (see Chapter 9)
> 9 premade sugar eyes

1. Roll out the red fondant until ⅛" thick and cut out a round with the cutter.
2. Cut a straight line across it 1⅜" from the top to make the bandana. Then cut 2 thin, long triangles to look like the bandana's knot/tie. Press the half circle onto the top of the pie using a tiny amount of water to adhere if necessary and the 2 triangles at one side with the larger ends touching the edge of the half-circle bandana.
3. Take a small piece of black fondant and roll it out like a long log to make a thin strap about 2" long. Press it onto the pie starting about halfway across the head and draping down to the side to look like the strap of an eyepatch. Roll another small piece of black fondant into a small ball and then press flat to make an eyepatch, stick onto the pirate head pie across the strap where the eye should be. Roll another small piece of black fondant into a thin log about 1" long and shape into a smile, press on where the pirate pie's mouth should be.
4. Pop the white Royal Icing into a small Ziploc bag and cut a tiny hole in the corner to make an easy disposable piping bag. Using the Royal Icing, stick the premade eye into place and then pipe lots of tiny dots onto the red fondant bandana to appear like polka dots.
5. Allow to dry and once set you can eat straight away of store in an airtight container for a couple of days.

Pirate Pie Pops

CHAPTER 7

Fruit on a Stick

Nutritious and delicious will be the kids favorite saying as they assemble these scrummy sweets. There are quite a few variations included, but once they get started the kids can come up with their own fruity creations using whatever is in season.

It's a good idea to use wooden sticks as fruit has a high water content and may make the paper-based lollipop sticks turn a bit soggy.

Grape, Cantaloupe, and Berry Skewers

Makes 12

These bright and sweet fruit skewers are packed with juicy goodness and delicious to boot. It's a great idea to eat a wide variety of brightly colored fruits and vegetables each day, and with these skewers you'll be off to a great start.

24 green grapes, seedless

1 cantaloupe

24 blueberries

1. Wash the grapes and blueberries and pat dry with absorbent towels.
2. Cut up the cantaloupe, remove the skin and seeds, and cut into cubes of around ¾".
3. Place a piece of cantaloupe on the wooden skewer, pushing down until it is a couple of inches from the top, and then add a blueberry and a grape. Repeat the pattern once, and then finish with a piece of cantaloupe.
4. Store any extra cantaloupe in an airtight container in the fridge and eat within a couple of days. Fruit skewers are best eaten the day they're made.

Deep-Freeze Chocolate Bananas

Makes 8

Ditch the store-bought frozen pops and try these homemade fresh fruit treats. They're packed with vitamins, but the kids don't have to know that. With the bit of added chocolate, they think they're just getting a treat!

4 bananas

10 ounces chocolate candy coating

Cornstarch

1. Line a tray with parchment paper.
2. Cut banana in half and pop into the freezer on the parchment-lined tray for an hour or until frozen.
3. Melt the candy coating in the microwave at medium low in 60-second bursts, stirring in between each burst. Repeat for a total of 3–5 minutes until the mixture is smooth.
4. Remove all the bananas from the freezer. Insert a wooden skewer into the cut half of a banana, pushing it halfway into the fruit.
5. Roll the banana in a little cornstarch and then dip into the melted chocolate. Tap to remove a little of the excess chocolate. The chocolate will set quickly, as the banana is frozen, so hold a moment until set. Return to the parchment paper and the freezer, or eat right away.

POP TIP

SPRINKLE WITH CRUSHED NUTS OR COCONUT FOR SOME VARIETY.

Frozen Berry Blasts

Makes 8

A great treat for hot summery days when you want to fill the kids with natural vitamins instead of sugar.

24 blueberries
24 raspberries
24 blackberries

1. Line a tray with aluminum foil.
2. Very gently rinse all berries and lay on absorbent towels to dry.
3. Place the berries onto the skewers in a pattern—blueberry, raspberry, blackberry, so you end up with 3 of each berry type on each skewer.
4. Place the skewers onto a tray lined with foil and pop into the freezer for half an hour. Serve the same day.

Red, White, and Blue Kabobs

Makes 12

Patriotic fruit kabobs are just the thing to take along to an outdoor picnic. If you can find white star-shaped marshmallows, use them in place of regular ones. You'll need 60 star marshmallows in total so make sure you get enough.

48 cherries
48 blueberries
30 white marshmallows

1. Gently wash the cherries and blueberries and pat dry with absorbent towels.
2. Remove the seed from each cherry carefully, using a cherry pitter. If you don't have a cherry pitter, you can remove the seed with a lollipop stick by carefully poking through the cherry until you hit the seed, removing the stick, and then pushing the lollipop stick in the opposite side of the cherry and pushing and wiggling until the seed loosens and falls out the first hole you made. Cut each marshmallow in half using safety scissors (do not cut star-shaped marshmallows).
3. Thread a white marshmallow onto the wooden skewer, followed by 2 cherries. Push all toward the bottom of the skewer.
4. Thread on another marshmallow, followed by 2 blueberries. Repeat the sequence of marshmallows and fruits, and finish off with a marshmallow.
5. Repeat for the remaining skewers. Chill until ready to serve. The fruit kabobs are best eaten the same day.

Rainbow Fruit Kabobs

Makes 12

Mouthfuls of juicy natural fruit combine in this kabob to create a rainbow party taste sensation. If any of the fruit is out of season, substitute a different type of the same color.

> 12 blueberries
> 12 purple grapes
> 12 raspberries
> 1 orange
> 2 kiwifruit
> ½ pineapple

1. Wash the blueberries and grapes and carefully pat dry with absorbent towels. Gently rinse the raspberries and lay on absorbent towels to air dry.
2. Peel the orange and kiwifruit and cut into pieces so you have 12 pieces of each fruit.
3. Peel the pineapple, remove the core, and cut off 12 even chunks around 1" in size.
4. Gently push the fruit onto the wooden skewer in the following order: grape, blueberry, kiwifruit, pineapple, orange, and raspberry.
5. Chill until ready to serve. Fruit skewers are best eaten the day they're made. Store any excess cut fruit in an airtight container in the fridge and eat within a couple of days.

Kool Kiwi Discs

Makes 16

Chocolate is a perfect match for a variety of fruits, and once you pop your fruit onto a stick, it's so easy to dip. Once you start dipping fruit, you'll be hooked. Try out this recipe with other fruits, like strawberries or raspberries.

4 kiwifruit

8 ounces white candy coating

Wooden paddle pop sticks

¼ cup cornstarch

1. Place absorbent paper towel in the bottom of an airtight container.
2. Peel kiwifruit and slice into 4 even discs. Pat dry with additional absorbent towels to absorb extra juice.
3. Melt white candy coating in a microwave-safe bowl at medium low heat in 60-second bursts, stirring after each burst. Repeat for 3–5 minutes until all the candy coating is melted.
4. Dip the end of a wooden stick into the candy coating and insert the stick into the edge of a kiwifruit disc. Lay the fruit onto the absorbent-paper-lined airtight container. Repeat the process for all of the discs and pop into the fridge to set.
5. Line a tray with parchment paper.
6. Remelt the candy coating. Remove the fruit from the fridge. Holding the end of the wooden stick, dip a whole kiwifruit disc into cornstarch until lightly covered and then the melted candy coating. Allow the excess candy coating to drip off and then lay the coated fruit disc onto the parchment paper to set.
7. Store in an airtight container in the fridge until required. This treat is best eaten the same day.

Strawberry Mallow Skewers

Makes 8

These fluffy sweet sticks won't last long. Try to purchase containers with even-size strawberries to make the skewers nicely balanced.

24 strawberries

16 large marshmallows

1. Wash strawberries, pat dry with absorbent towels, and remove the leaves.
2. Place strawberries on the skewers alternatively with marshmallow until you have 3 strawberries and 2 marshmallows on each skewer. Serve the same day.

Dip-and-Dunk Fruit

Serves 12

Have trouble getting the kids to eat fruit? This serve-yourself fruit feast is sure to tempt. Use the fruit suggested or any combination of your favorite fruit.

> 1 pint strawberries
> ½ pint blueberries
> 3 bananas
> 4 kiwifruit
> ½ cantaloupe
> ½ cup chocolate sprinkles
> 1 cup cripsy rice cereal or Reese's Puffs
> ½ cup crushed nuts
> 1 batch Marshmallow Dipping Sauce (see Chapter 9)

1. Wash and hull the strawberries (remove the leaves), wash the blueberries, and leave on absorbent towels to dry.
2. Peel the banana and cut into bite-size slices.
3. Remove the skin from the kiwifruit and cantaloupe and cut into bite-size pieces.
4. Arrange the fruit on a plate. Put the sprinkles, crispy rice cereal or Reese's Puffs, and crushed nuts in separate small bowls with a spoon in each. Spoon the marshmallow sauce into a medium-size bowl. Set out the skewers.
5. Have everyone serve themselves by placing a piece of fruit on the end of the skewer, dipping it into the marshmallow sauce, and sprinkling on some of the toppings.

Crazy Tropo Fruit Treats

Makes 12

The kids will think you've moved to a tropical island when you start preparations for these cool, summery fruit skewers.

> ½ pineapple
> ½ papaya
> 2 bananas
> 1 mango
> 1 cup vanilla yogurt
> 2 tablespoons honey
> 1 tablespoon shredded coconut

1. Peel all the fruit, remove seeds, and cut into 1" chunks.
2. Pour the yogurt into a bowl and swirl the honey into the top. Sprinkle with the coconut.
3. Let the kids push the fruit randomly onto the skewers to make their own tropical creations, dipping the skewers in the yogurt for a finishing touch. Best eaten immediately.

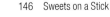

Candy Apples

Makes 8

The candy coating needs to be heated to a very high temperature, so it is not suitable for small children to help. However, they can still help out washing and drying the apples and inserting the wooden skewers. Older kids will be able to dip the apples in the candy mixture. Make sure the mixture reaches 300°F, or the candy coating will not set.

8 medium red apples

Thick wooden skewers either round pointed or paddle type

2¾ cups sugar

1¼ cups corn syrup

1½ cups water

Red food color

1 teaspoon vanilla extract

1. Grease a large baking pan.
2. Wash and dry the apples, remove the stems, and insert a wooden skewer into the bottom of each apple, about ⅔ of the way through the fruit.
3. Combine the sugar, corn syrup, and water in a medium saucepan at low heat, stirring constantly.
4. Increase the heat to high, continuing to stir until the mixture starts to boil. Then let it continue to boil without stirring until it reaches 300°F on a candy thermometer.
5. Remove mixture from heat and add food color until the candy coating reaches the color you desire. Once the mixture stops bubbling, add the vanilla extract and stir until combined.
6. Working quickly, dip each apple into the candy coating, swirling to cover the whole apple. If necessary, use a spoon to ensure the whole apple is covered.
7. Place apples in the greased baking pan to set.

POP TIP

TRY OTHER FLAVORS, LIKE CHERRY, IN PLACE OF VANILLA. SOME OF THE LEFTOVER CANDY COATING CAN BE MADE INTO FREEFORM LOLLIPOPS. JUST GREASE A TRAY, PLACE SOME LOLLIPOP STICKS ON THE TRAY, AND SPOON TABLESPOONS OF THE CANDY MIXTURE OVER THE TOP OF THE LOLLIPOP STICKS.

Candy Apples

Fruity Flowers

Makes 12

Fruit pretending to be a flower, what fun! Use metal cutters instead of plastic for these as the thinner edge slices through the fruit easier. Make sure you keep all the extra pieces to make up a scrumptious fruit salad.

3 slices watermelon, ½" thick

2" flower-shape cookie cutter

¾" round fondant cutter

1 slice cantaloupe, ½" thick

12 green grapes

1. Lay the watermelon onto a cutting board. Using the flower-shape cutter, push down to make watermelon flowers.
2. Use the ¾" round cutter to cut a hole out of the center of each watermelon flower.
3. Lay the cantaloupe on the cutting board and use the ¾" cutter to make 12 rounds.
4. To assemble, place the cantaloupe round in the hole inside the watermelon.
5. Push a grape onto a wooden skewer, inserting the skewer about ¼" from the edge and angling the grape up a little to look like a leaf.
6. Push the watermelon flower with the cantaloupe center onto the wooden skewer on top of the grape. Best served the same day.

Happy Halloween Caramel Apples

Makes 6

Here is a super-easy way to make your own caramel apples. Pick the freshest apples you can find for these treats. Remember that the caramel will be hot when it comes out of the microwave, so supervision is essential. Younger kids will be able to help by preparing the apples and unwrapping the caramels.

6 small to medium green apples

Thick wooden skewers

14-ounce bag of caramels

2 tablespoons milk

1. Line a baking tray with aluminum foil and grease the foil with a little oil.
2. Wash and dry the apples, remove the stems, and insert the wooden skewers in the bottom of each apple, about ⅔ of the way through the fruit.
3. Unwrap all the caramels and place them in a large microwave-safe bowl with the milk. Heat in the microwave at high heat for 60 seconds. Remove mixture from the microwave, stir, and then heat for another 60 seconds on high. Stir and leave to cool slightly.
4. Dip each apple into the caramel mixture, using a spoon to make sure the apples are completely covered.
5. Place on prepared tray and allow to cool and set.

ROLL THE BOTTOMS OF THE APPLES INTO CRUSHED NUTS FOR EXTRA CRUNCH.

Chocolate-Wrapped Caramel Apples

Makes 6

Add another whole layer to your caramel apples by dipping in chocolate and your favorite candy bar. If you like, you can replace the candy bar with Halloween sprinkles or cereal.

- 6 caramel apples on sticks (premade or make your own Happy Halloween Caramel Apples using the recipe in this chapter)
- 2 cups candy bars of your choice (any type), chopped in small pieces
- 14 ounces candy coating
- 2 tablespoons Crisco or other vegetable shortening

1. Line a baking tray with parchment paper.
2. Spread the chopped candy bars over the surface of a large plate.
3. In a large microwave-safe dish, melt the candy coating with the shortening at medium low in short bursts of 60 seconds each, stirring in between each burst for a total of 4–6 minutes, until all the coating is smooth and lump free.
4. Holding the end of a candy apple stick, dip the apple in the melted candy coating. Use a spoon to quickly cover the apple with the melted candy. Pull the apple out of the melted candy and hold it over the bowl to let some of the excess candy drip off.
5. Working quickly, place the candy-coated apple on top of the chopped candy bars. Using your hands, sprinkle candy pieces around the sides evenly.
6. Place the apple onto the parchment paper to set. Repeat the process for all of the apples.

 POP TIP

USE WHITE OR PINK CANDY COATING AND HEART SPRINKLES TO MAKE SUGARY-SWEET VALENTINE CARAMEL APPLES.

◆ ◆ ◆

# Apricot Balls

Makes 14

Naturally sweet ingredients combine to create a perfect take anywhere treat. Chopping the apricots with safety scissors is a great activity to keep little ones occupied and involved.

- 8½ ounces dried apricots, chopped
- 1¼ cup shredded coconut
- 1½ tablespoons honey
- 2 ounces white candy coating

1. Line a tray with parchment paper.
2. Combine apricots, coconut, and honey in a large bowl. Mix well.
3. Wet hands and roll 1½-teaspoon amounts of the mixture into small balls. Set on the parchment-lined tray. Repeat for remaining mixture and place in fridge to chill.
4. Melt the candy coating in a small microwave-safe dish at short bursts of 60 seconds at medium low in the microwave until melted. Dip the end of a stick into the melted candy and push the stick into the top of each of the balls; press the mixture in around the pop firmly. Return to parchment-lined tray and pop back into fridge to chill for 30 minutes. Store in an airtight container up to a week.

Bitty Banana Split Bites

Makes 12

Fake little banana splits are a hoot to make and eat, and are lick-smackingly cute.

12 cherries

4 ounces chocolate candy coating

3 bananas

Rainbow sprinkles

36 mini marshmallow

1 tablespoon crushed nuts

1 cup Vanilla Buttercream Frosting (see Chapter 2)

1. Wash and dry the cherries.
2. Melt the candy coating in a microwave-safe bowl on medium low in 60 second bursts, stirring after each burst until the candy is melted.
3. Peel and cut each banana into 4 pieces. Push a piece of banana onto a wooden skewer so it's just at the tip. Dip the tip of the banana into the melted candy, move the banana away from the bowl, and then gently shake some of the rainbow sprinkles over the coated banana.
4. Working quickly before the candy coating sets, pop 3 mini marshmallows and ¼ teaspoon of crushed nuts onto the the top of candy-covered banana.
5. Place the skewer into a Styrofoam block to set.
6. Place the buttercream frosting into a piping bag with a star tip or in a Ziploc bag with a medium hole cut out of one corner. Pipe a swirl of buttercream on top of the marshmallow-topped bananas. Top each skewer with a cherry and serve immediately.

Cranberry and White Chocolate Clusters

Makes 12

Scrumptious dried fruit enrobed in chocolate on a pop make a dainty little treat. Try replacing the cranberries with other favorite fruits, like dried cherries, or add some nuts.

10 ounces white candy coating or white chocolate
1 cup dried cranberries

1. Line a tray with parchment paper. Lay out 12 lollipop sticks on the tray, spacing them a couple of inches apart.
2. Melt the candy coating in a large microwave-safe bowl at medium low for 60-second bursts, stirring between each burst for a total of 4–6 minutes, until the mixture is smooth and lump free.
3. Using a large spoon, stir the cranberries and nuts (if using) into the melted candy coating.
4. Spoon heaped tablespoons of the mixture carefully onto the tops of the lollipop sticks. Gently jiggle and turn the sticks without picking them up just to make sure they are encased in the mixture. Leave to set at room temperature.

Apple "Cupcakes"

Makes 8

These super-cool-looking fake cupcakes are great for summer when you don't want to heat up the kitchen. If you're pressed for time, you can just use smooth peanut butter in place of the frosting.

4 medium apples
1 cup Peanut Butter Frosting (see Chapter 9)
2 tablespoons rainbow sprinkles

1. Wash and dry the apples. Remove the stems and cut in half.
2. Spread the frosting on the cut top of each apple and sprinkle with the rainbow sprinkles.
3. Insert a wooden skewer into the bottom of each apple. Carefully holding the sides of the apple, insert the skewer about ¾".
4. Place the skewers into a Styrofoam block to hold the "cupcake" upright.

INSTEAD OF SPRINKLES USE RAISINS, RICE KRISPIES, OR ANOTHER CEREAL.

CHAPTER 8

Candy on a Stick

Everyone loves candy, and your tempting confections will seem even more delightful and unique when served up on a stick. These recipes have been chosen to provide maximum yummi-ness while remaining easy for younger chefs to master.

Anything Goes Candy Pops

Makes 12

This is a great way to use up any extra candy coating you have left over after dipping other treats. Go crazy with the decorations and use a variety of sprinkles, premade sugar decorations, chopped candy bars, or even small cookies, like tiny teddies.

4 ounces candy coating (any color)
Wooden craft sticks
¼ cup sprinkles or decorations of choice

1. Line a tray with parchment paper.
2. In a microwave-safe bowl, melt the candy coating by heating at medium low in 60-second bursts, stirring in between bursts for a total of 4–6 minutes, until all the coating is smooth and lump free.
3. Spoon 1 teaspoon of melted candy coating onto the parchment-lined tray. Press the end of a wooden stick into the melted candy, and then spoon another teaspoon of candy on top. Using the back of a spoon, smooth the melted candy into a round.
4. Sprinkle ½ to 1 teaspoon of sprinkles on top of the melted candy. Leave to set on the parchment paper. Store in an airtight container for up to 2 weeks.

Anything Goes Candy Pops

Creamy
Dreamy
White
Chocolate
Fudge

Beyond
Chocolate
Fudge Bite

Oreo
Truffle
Pop

Beyond Chocolate Fudge Bites

Makes around 30

Making this microwave fudge is a cinch. In fact, it's so easy to make and delicious that you may need to hide the instructions from the kids, or they won't stop making it.

- 3 11½-ounce bags (2 pounds 2½ ounces) chocolate chips
- 1 14-ounce can condensed milk
- 1 teaspoon vanilla
- 14 ounces white candy coating

1. Line an 8" × 8" baking pan with aluminum foil.
2. Place chocolate and condensed milk in a microwave-safe bowl and heat at medium for 30 seconds. Remove and stir. Continue to heat for 30-second intervals until all the chocolate is melted. Mix in vanilla.
3. Chill in fridge for about 1 hour until set, or at room temperature for a few hours. Turn out on a cutting board lined with parchment paper. Cut into shapes or cubes. Place onto a parchment-lined tray and return to fridge.
4. In a large microwave-safe bowl, melt the candy coating by heating at medium low in 60-second bursts, stirring in between bursts for a total of 4–6 minutes, until all the coating is smooth and lump free. Dip the end of a stick into the candy and then push the stick into one of the fudge bites. Repeat for all of the fudge. Return to parchment-lined tray and pop back into fridge to chill for 10 minutes.
5. Remelt the candy coating if necessary. Remove tray from fridge. Holding the end of the stick, dip each fudge bite into the melted candy. Remove excess candy coating by gently tapping the stick on the edge of the bowl. Return to the parchment-lined tray to set.

POP TIP

SPRINKLE THE DIPPED FUDGE BITES WITH FINELY CRUSHED OREO COOKIES BEFORE THE CHOCOLATE HAS SET.

Creamy Dreamy White Chocolate Fudge

Makes around 25

All your sweet candy dreams will come true with these heavenly bites of white chocolate covered in dark chocolate candy coating.

2 cups (12 ounces) white chocolate chips
¼ stick (1 ounce) unsalted butter
1 14-ounce can condensed milk
14 ounces chocolate candy coating

1. Line an 8" × 8" baking pan with aluminum foil.
2. Place white chocolate chips, butter, and condensed milk in a microwave-safe bowl and heat at medium for 30 seconds. Remove and stir. Continue to heat for 30-second intervals until all the chocolate is melted.
3. Chill in fridge for about 1 hour until set or at room temperature for a few hours. Turn out on a cutting board lined with parchment paper and cut into shapes or into cubes. Place onto a parchment-lined baking tray and return to fridge.
4. In a large microwave-safe bowl, melt the candy coating by heating at medium low in 60-second bursts, stirring in between bursts for a total of 4–6 minutes, until all the coating is smooth and lump free. Dip the end of a stick into the candy and then push the stick into one of the white chocolate fudge bites. Repeat for all of the fudge. Return to parchment-lined tray and pop back into fridge to chill for 10 minutes.
5. Remelt the candy coating if necessary. Remove tray from fridge. Holding the end of the stick, dip each fudge bite into the melted candy. Remove excess candy coating by gently tapping the stick on the edge of the bowl. Return to the parchment-lined tray to set.

POP TIP

FOR A CHRISTMAS TREAT, CRUSH PEPPERMINT CANDY CANES AND SPRINKLE OVER THE FUDGE BITES BEFORE THE CHOCOLATE HAS SET.

Makes around 25

The name says it all really. This peanut butter fudge on a stick will have you in a state of bliss with just one bite.

3 cups (18 ounces) semisweet chocolate chips
1 can condensed milk
½ stick (2 ounces) unsalted butter
½ cup peanut butter
14 ounces chocolate candy coating

1. Line an 8" × 8" baking pan with aluminum foil.
2. Place chocolate chips, condensed milk, butter, and peanut butter into a large microwave-safe bowl and heat at medium for 30 seconds. Remove and stir. Continue to heat for 30-second intervals until all the chocolate is melted.
3. Pour into pan and level top with the back of a spoon.
4. Chill in fridge for about 1 hour until set or at room temperature for a few hours. Turn out on a cutting board lined with parchment paper and cut into shapes or into cubes. Place onto a parchment-lined baking tray and return to fridge.
5. In a large microwave-safe bowl, melt the candy coating by heating at medium low in 60-second bursts, stirring in between bursts for a total of 4–6 minutes, until all the coating is smooth and lump free. Dip the end of a stick into the candy and then push the stick into one of the peanut butter bites. Repeat for all of the peanut butter fudge. Return to parchment-lined tray and pop back into fridge to chill for 10 minutes.
6. Remelt the candy coating if necessary. Remove tray from fridge. Holding the end of the stick, dip each peanut butter bite into the melted candy. Remove excess candy coating by gently tapping the stick on the edge of the bowl. Return to the parchment-lined tray to set.

Coconut Ice Easter Eggs

Makes 36

Start a tradition of making Coconut Ice Easter Eggs every year. This recipe will become a household favorite.

- 1 14-ounce can condensed milk
- 3¼ cups powdered sugar, sifted
- 3 cups shredded coconut
- 1 teaspoon vanilla
- Yellow, blue, and pink gel food color
- 14 ounces candy coating

1. Line a tray with parchment paper.
2. Mix the condensed milk, powdered sugar, shredded coconut, and vanilla until well combined.
3. Divide mixture into 3 portions and tint each a different color.
4. Roll a piece of coconut mixture about the size of a Ping-Pong ball in your palm until the sides are smooth and the mixture resembles an egg. Place each egg on the tray lined with parchment paper and leave to harden slightly, about 1 hour.
5. In a large microwave-safe bowl, melt the candy coating by heating at medium low in 60-second bursts, stirring in between bursts for a total of 4–6 minutes, until all the coating is smooth and lump free. Dip the end of a stick into the candy, and then push the stick into the larger end of an egg. Repeat for all of the eggs. Allow to set at room temperature for an hour.
6. Remelt the candy coating. Holding the end of the stick, dip a coconut egg into the melted candy until the whole shape is submerged, and then lift it out of the melted candy. Holding the pop over the bowl to catch drips, gently tap the stick against your hand or the side of the bowl to remove excess candy coating. Remove as much excess as possible before you put the pop into a Styrofoam block.
7. Repeat for remaining pops and leave to set.

POP TIP

IF YOU LIKE, YOU CAN MAKE "REAL"-LOOKING EGGS COMPLETE WITH YOLKS. COLOR ¼ OF THE MIXTURE YELLOW TO LOOK LIKE THE COLOR OF AN EGG YOLK (LEAVE THE REST OF THE MIXTURE WHITE). TAKE A PIECE OF THE YELLOW MIXTURE ABOUT THE SIZE OF A PENNY AND ROLL IT BETWEEN YOUR PALMS UNTIL ROUND.

FLATTEN A PIECE OF THE UNCOLORED MIXTURE THE SIZE OF A PING-PONG BALL AND WRAP IT AROUND THE YELLOW "YOLK" CENTER. ROLL THE MIXTURE IN YOUR PALM TO MAKE A SMOOTH EGG SHAPE AND THEN DIP ACCORDING TO THE RECIPE INSTRUCTIONS.

Haystacks on a Pitchfork

Makes 16

Chocolate stacked with coconut makes a glorious combination. If you have trouble locating the wooden forks, don't worry—these treats taste just as good on a regular wooden paddle pop craft stick.

> 14 ounces candy coating (any color)
> 2 cups shredded coconut
> 16 disposable-type wooden forks

1. Line 2 trays with parchment paper.
2. In a microwave-safe bowl, melt the candy coating by heating at medium low in 60-second bursts, stirring in between bursts for a total of 4–6 minutes, until all the coating is smooth and lump free.
3. Remove from microwave and stir in the shredded coconut until well combined.
4. Working quickly, before the candy melt has time to set, dollop about 3 teaspoons of the mixture onto the parchment paper. Insert a wooden fork into the side of the coconut stack and press down lightly to ensure it is secure.
5. Leave to set on the parchment-lined tray.

Peanut Candy Clusters

Makes 16

Glorious chunky bites reminiscent of candy bars make a perfect gift for anyone who loves peanuts. You can use Reese's Pieces in place of the peanut butter chips if you would like to add a little color to the mix.

> 14 ounces milk chocolate
> ½ cup unsalted roasted peanuts
> ½ cup peanut butter chips
> Wooden paddle pop craft sticks

1. Line a tray with parchment paper.
2. In a large microwave-safe bowl, melt the chocolate by heating at medium low in 60-second bursts, stirring in between bursts for a total of 4–6 minutes, until all the coating is smooth and lump free.
3. Add the peanuts and peanut butter chips and mix until coated.
4. Working quickly, before the chocolate sets, spoon a tablespoon of the mixture onto the parchment-lined tray. Press in a wooden stick and then top with another tablespoon of mixture. Repeat until all mixture is used.
5. Allow to set on the tray. Store in an airtight container for up to 1 week.

Fairy Bite Marshmallow Pops

Makes 18

Perk up your marshmallows with a little fairy magic pizzazz. Oh, and some sugar sprinkles, of course. This sweet treat on a stick gives maximum impact for minimal effort and is just the thing for beginning decorators.

10 ounces pink candy coating
18 marshmallows
Pink and or purple sprinkles

1. Line a tray with parchment paper.
2. In a microwave-safe bowl, melt the candy coating by heating at medium low in 60-second bursts, stirring in between bursts for a total of 4–6 minutes, until all the coating is smooth and lump free.
3. Dip the end of the lollipop sticks into the melted candy and insert into the marshmallows. Allow to set for 10 minutes.
4. Remelt the candy coating if necessary. Holding the end of the stick, dip the top of a marshmallow into the melted candy and then lift it out. Holding the pop over the bowl to catch drips, gently tap the stick against your hand or the side of the bowl to remove excess candy coating.
5. Move the pop away from the bowl. Working quickly, before the candy sets, shake the sprinkles over the candy-coated marshmallow. Stick the pop upright into a Styrofoam block to set. Repeat for remaining pops.

Fairy Bite Marshmallow Pops

Rocky Road Mountains

Makes 12

These mounds of candy are huge and yummy. If the kiddies are too young to eat nuts, leave them out completely or substitute dried fruit or a chopped candy bar.

2 cups marshmallows
2¼ cups (14 ounces) semisweet or milk chocolate chips
½ cup roasted unsalted peanuts
½ cup shredded coconut
Wooden paddle pop sticks

1. Line a tray with parchment paper.
2. Cut the marshmallows into quarters (if using mini marshmallows, you can skip this step).
3. In a large microwave-safe bowl, melt the chocolate by heating at medium low in 60-second bursts, stirring in between bursts for a total of 4–6 minutes, until all the coating is smooth and lump free.
4. Stir in the marshmallows, peanuts, and coconut. Mix until coated with chocolate.
5. Spoon mounds about ¼ cup in size onto the parchment-lined tray.
6. Push a wooden stick into the top of each mound and leave to set.

MAKE SNOWY MOUNTAINS BY REPLACING THE SEMISWEET CHOCOLATE WITH WHITE CHOCOLATE AND USING DRIED CHERRIES IN PLACE OF THE PEANUTS.

CHAPTER 9

The Icing on the Cake

A collection of sweet finishing touches that will take you from frosting cupcakes and decorating cookies to making cake pops the delicious treats they are. Don't be constrained by the suggestions in this book; mix and match these frostings to come up with new favorite taste sensations. All the frostings or buttercreams are best used immediately, but they can be stored for 2 days in an airtight container in the fridge and then brought back to room temperature to use as a cake pop ingredient. If you do want to store and then use as a frosting, you will need to bring back to room temperature and then beat with a mixer for a couple of minutes to fluff the ingredients back up prior to using.

Cream Cheese Frosting

Makes 1¼ cups

This Cream Cheese Frosting is perfect just as it is, but if you like a little zing, add a couple of teaspoons of lemon zest and mix well. Suitable both for cupcakes and to mix into cake pop mixture.

- ½ stick (2 ounces) unsalted butter at room temperature
- 4 ounces cream cheese at room temperature
- 2 cups powdered sugar, sifted
- ½ teaspoon vanilla extract

1. In the bowl of a mixer combine the butter and cream cheese at medium speed. Reduce speed to low and mix in the powdered sugar and vanilla. Increase to high speed and continue mixing for 3 minutes or until the frosting is light and fluffy.

Raspberry Buttercream

Makes 2 cups

Tangy raspberry combines with sweet frosting to make a luscious fruit-laden topping that is suitable to use for delicious cupcakes or as a cake pop mix add-in.

- ½ cup fresh raspberries (or frozen, defrosted)
- 1 stick (4 ounces) unsalted butter at room temperature
- 1 teaspoon vanilla extract
- ⅛ teaspoon salt
- 3 cups powdered sugar, sifted

1. Lightly wash raspberries and allow to dry on absorbent towels.
2. In the bowl of a mixer combine the butter, raspberries, vanilla, and salt. Mix at high speed until well combined and creamy.
3. Add the powdered sugar 1 cup at a time, mixing well after each addition.

Peanut Butter Frosting

Makes 2 cups

Be careful with this frosting—it's so good you might eat it all up before you get a chance to use it. Suitable to use for frosting cupcakes and as an add-in to a cake pop mixture.

1 stick (4 ounces) unsalted butter at room temperature
4 ounces cream cheese at room temperature
½ cup smooth peanut butter
2 cups powdered sugar, sifted

1. In the bowl of a mixer combine the butter and cream cheese at medium speed. Add the peanut butter and mix until just combined.
2. Reduce speed to low and mix in the powdered sugar. Increase to high speed and continue mixing for 3 minutes or until the frosting is light and fluffy.

◆ ◆ ◆

Royal Icing

Makes 1½ cups

This sugary icing sets hard and is perfect for adding details or using like a glue to stick on decorations. Royal Icing can easily be colored using gel food color. Add color in a drop at a time until the desired color is achieved. Dark colors like red or black should be made up the night before you want to use them.

2 tablespoons meringue powder
2 cups powdered sugar
4 tablespoons warm water

1. Place all ingredients in a bowl and mix at high speed until stiff peaks form. This will take a few minutes.
2. Use within a couple of days. Store in an airtight container with a layer of plastic wrap covering the surface of the icing. When ready to use, add any colors desired and then add water ½ teaspoon at a time until you have achieved the consistency of thick syrup.

◆ ◆ ◆

Chocolate Icing

Makes 1 cup

This sweet glaze topping is perfect for when something simple is called for, but it is not suitable for adding to cake pop mix.

2 cups powdered sugar, sifted
2 tablespoons unsweetened cocoa
1–2 tablespoons milk

1. Sift together the sugar and cocoa in a medium bowl. Add 1 tablespoon milk, and mix until combined. If required, continue to add milk 1 teaspoon at a time until the mixture is spreadable.

Marshmallow Fondant

Makes 22 ounces

Make your own fondant for covering cookies and making amazing decorations. It isn't as tricky to use as it seems. If the kids are a whizzes with Play-Doh, let them give this a try. The process for mixing up the Marshmallow Fondant is pretty sticky, so make sure you cover up with aprons if you have them handy. If your not keen on making your own, you can buy ready-made Wilton fondant to replace Marshmallow Fondant in any of the recipes in this book.

8 ounces white mini marshmallows
1½ cups powdered sugar, sifted
Crisco or other vegetable shortening
2 teaspoons water

1. Place marshmallows and water in a large microwave-safe bowl (this is going to get messy and sticky). Melt at high in 30-second increments for a total of 2 minutes, stirring at each 30-second interval. CAUTION: the marshmallow mixture will be very hot and sticky, so this step is not suitable for very young children.
2. Add powdered sugar and mix well with a spoon. Be very careful, as the marshmallow mixture will be very hot.
3. Grease the work surface and everyone's hands *very* well with Crisco, and have more ready to regrease as necessary. Any hard work surface like a kitchen bench should be suitable.
4. Knead the Marshmallow Fondant until smooth and stretchable. If the fondant begins to tear, add ½ teaspoon water at a time and knead again.
5. Wrap in plastic wrap and refrigerate overnight. Microwave for 10 seconds when ready to use.
6. Store in an airtight container at room temperature. To use, roll out on a surface lightly sprinkled with corn starch.

POP TIP

TO COLOR MARSHMALLOW FONDANT, KNEAD IN GEL FOOD COLOR UNTIL IT IS WELL BLENDED. IF YOU ARE COLORING THE WHOLE BATCH OF FONDANT JUST ONE COLOR, YOU CAN ADD ABOUT ¼ TEASPOON OF COLOR IMMEDIATELY AFTER YOU ADD YOUR POWDERED SUGAR AND THEN KNEAD IN WELL. ADD MORE COLOR AS REQUIRED. RED AND OTHER DARK COLORS MAY NEED QUITE A BIT MORE. IF YOU NEED DIFFERENT COLORS FROM THE SAME BATCH, THE COLOR CAN BE ADDED AT ANY TIME AFTER THE INITIAL KNEADING BY DIVIDING THE FONDANT INTO REQUIRED PORTIONS, ADDING THE GEL COLOR, AND KNEADING UNTIL WELL COMBINED.

Marshmallow Dipping Sauce

Makes 1½ cups

This super-easy Marshmallow Dipping Sauce is delicious served with any of the fruit pops. For a extra little zing, you can add 1 tablespoon of orange juice and a little grated orange zest.

8 ounces cream cheese at room temperature
7 ounces marshmallow creme or fluff

1. In a large bowl mix cream cheese and marshmallow creme together until combined and no lumps remain.
2. Keep covered in fridge until ready for use. Best served the same day.

Chocolate Dipping Sauce

Makes 1⅓ cups

Rich and chocolaty, this sauce is super-quick to make, so you can start dipping and eating those sweets on a stick even faster.

½ cup heavy cream
7 ounces milk chocolate or semisweet chocolate

1. Place the cream and chocolate in a large microwave-safe bowl and heat at medium low in 90-second bursts, stirring in between each burst, until melted.
2. The sauce will keep in an airtight container in the refrigerator for up to 3 days. Reheat before using.

Edible Paint

Makes 1½ cups

While not a food in itself, this homemade Edible Paint can be used to decorate fondant-covered cookies. When painting on food items that you are planning to eat, make sure you use new brushes or ones that have only been used for other food items in the past. You do not want to introduce any non-foodsafe particles into your treats!

½ cup cornstarch
1½ cups water
½ teaspoon salt
3 tablespoons sugar
Assortment of gel food colors

1. Place cornstarch, water, salt, and sugar into a small saucepan and heat at medium low until the mixture thickens to a gluelike consistency.
2. Divide into portions and color with food color as desired.

CHAPTER 10

Decorating and Displaying Your Pops

There are so many different ways to decorate your sweet treats on a stick. You can let the kids' and your own creativity run wild. Check out your craft box, toy box, and pantry for decorations and display ideas. Be inspired by the treats you are displaying, and most of all have fun.

Decorating Your Lollipop Sticks

Plain lollipop sticks are fine for everyday eating but some occasions call for a bit of razzle dazzle. To get you started, here are some ideas to add the finishing touch to your fun treat.

Ribbons

Tie ribbons in bows around the tops of lollipop sticks or skewers to give the sticks a quick lift. Try to choose colors and patterns that match the theme of your pop; for example, gingham for cowboy theme, black and orange for Halloween. Craft and discount stores have so many different types of ribbon to choose from that you are sure to find a perfect match. If you have trouble getting bows to look even, just tie short lengths of ribbon with a double knot rather than a real bow. Wand-type treats look great with longer lengths of ribbon hanging down so that the ribbon twirls around while the kids make magical spells. The curling ribbon that you use on presents can also look effective.

Paper Cut-Outs

You can decorate the sticks of pops, cookies, and other treats with cute paper cut-outs. Use a craft punch to cut out rounds, hearts, or other shapes of about 1½"–2½" and then make a hole at the top and another at the bottom, both about ¼" from the edge. Thread the lollipop stick through the holes and, if necessary, secure at the back with a little sticky tape.

Pretty paper for scrapbooking is available at craft and discount stores, and you can find a wide variety of downloadable printables online, both free and for purchase, that are suitable for this purpose.

Another fun idea is to draw body shapes for the pops or treats, cut them out freehand, and attach them to the stick using the same two-hole method. Some of the pops in this book that would be fun for trying out this idea include the Alien Invasion Pops, Pup Pops, and Leaping Laughing Frogs (all found in Chapter 2).

Cake Pop and Cupcake Toppers

Top off plain pops, cupcakes, and fudge with fun cardboard cupcake toppers shaped like princesses, pirates, other assorted fun figures, and even favorite cartoon and TV characters. Available from craft stores, specialty cake stores, and online, these toppers make decorating your sweets a cinch. If you're a whiz at crafts, you might even be able to make your own with cardstock and a wooden pick. Just insert the topper into the treat and transform it from fun to fabulous.

Decorated Masking Tape

There is a huge variety of decorative masking tape available with all manner of cute pictures from woodland themes to Alice in Wonderland and Little Red Riding Hood. Cut a length of tape and wrap it around the stick, joining the ends together to look like a little flag for an easy but funky finish.

Pipe Cleaners

Whether you need to create spider or bug legs or maybe even an octopus or jellyfish, pipe cleaners provide a simple way to add some 3-D excitement. Just cut

them to the required length, wrap them around the stick, and bend the pipe cleaners around to get the effect you are looking for.

Wooden Craft Stick Messages and Thank-You Notes

Write descriptive words like *chocolate* and *yum* and short messages like *Happy Birthday*, or draw decorative hearts on the ends of wooden craft sticks with nontoxic pens. This is easiest to do before you insert the sticks into your treat.

Treats on a stick, like cookie pops, can make a perfect take-home thank-you gift for a party. Craft pretty handmade or printable thank-you notes and tie on with some twine or ribbon.

How to Hold and Display Your Treats

For sweets on a stick with pizzazz, display a bunch together in a gorgeous container. They look great at parties as a centerpiece, and the best part is that you can eat them for dessert or hand them out as take-home gifts at the end of the party.

Pretty Pails, Flowerpots, Gift Boxes, and Planters

Craft and discount stores abound with containers in all the colors of the rainbow. At holiday times they even come in festive patterns. To display your pops in a container, cut a piece of Styrofoam to fit and push it in

securely. The trick to making the holder look complete is to cover the top so you cannot see the Styrofoam. If there are gaps between the Styrofoam and the container edges, stuff in a little bit of crumpled paper or plastic wrap to make the top even. Stick your pops into the Styrofoam and then cover the top with a decorative finish. You'll find a list of suggestions for the finishing touch at the end of this chapter.

Glass Jars and Vases

Filled with candy or other decorations to support the pops, these are a quick and simple solution to displaying your treats upright so all of your fabulous decorating work can shine. Make sure the container you choose has a heavy base so it will not tip over with the weight of the pops. If the container is opaque, you can add a weight into the bottom to make it more secure and then stick in Styrofoam to help hold the pops in place. Another trick is to stick a large clump of nontoxic adhesive putty to the inside of the jar. The putty will help to keep the pops in place, and you can move the candy around it to hide the putty from view.

3-D Pop-Up Cards

If you only need to display a few smaller pops or are looking for a lovely way to display your sweets for a gift, the 3-D pop-up cards made by companies like Russ available through Amazon and other suppliers will enhance any display. These types of cards have a square bottom with the decorative cardboard display fanning out with lots of little nooks and crannies that could be used to hold a treat (the ones used as centerpieces to hold balloons are perfect). To make them pop ready, secure a heavy weight inside at the bottom, then fill the holes with some nontoxic play dough colored to match the card. Take care when inserting your pops to space, and balance them evenly so the card will not easily tip over.

Play Dough

Make your own nontoxic play dough and color it any color you need. This can look great in solid colors or layered in glass jars, and you can even bury some toys or other decorations in it for extra fun. To make your own play dough, place ½ cup salt, 1 cup all-purpose flour, 2 tablespoons cream of tartar, 1 cup water, and 1 tablespoon vegetable oil into a saucepan and stir over medium-low heat until the mixture is pliable. Let the dough cool and then knead until smooth, adding food color as needed. If the play dough is too soft to hold up the pops, add in more all-purpose flour as required. Store it in Ziploc bags or airtight containers until you need to use it. Note: although this play dough is not toxic, it is not suitable to eat due to the high amount of salt.

Wooden Display Boxes

You can make a reusable wooden stand by drilling small holes into a thick round, square, or rectangle of wood with an ¹¹⁄₃₂" or ³⁄₁₆" drill bit (see which size you like for your pops by trying it out on some scrap wood).

Before you start drilling, make up a template on paper of where you would like the holes to go, then adhere the template to the wood with adhesive tape and drill through the paper template into the wood. Don't drill holes all the way through or your pops will slide down if you have to pick the display up to move it.

Once you have the holes where you need them, give the block a quick sanding and wipe it clean. Finish off with a coat or two of nontoxic paint.

If you're not really good with crafts or don't have suitable tools, you can buy ready-made wooden stands from a number of suppliers on Etsy.com.

Styrofoam Covered in Paper

One of the easiest ways to display your treats is a Styrofoam block neatly wrapped in pretty decorative paper to match your party theme or sweet treats. Make sure that the foam is tall and wide enough to be stable, and try to ensure that the folds of the paper and the tape you use are mostly hidden on the bottoms and sides. Once the block is covered, you can also decorate the sides with stickers or drawings if you like.

To minimize the risk of ripping the paper when you are inserting your treats, mark where each treat will be inserted with a pen and carefully poke holes through the paper and a couple of inches into the Styrofoam with a metal skewer.

The treats should be evenly spaced without touching each other when you have finished. A 12" × 12" block of foam can hold 36 cake pops. Styrofoam is available from craft stores and online.

Fresh Fruit

Serving fruit kabobs? Nature has come up with the perfect decorative centerpiece for you. Use a pineapple, watermelon, or other sturdy fruit to stick the skewers into. If you are cutting the fruit in half, lay it onto a plate cut-side down to capture any juice.

Lollipop and Cake Pop Stand

A number of companies now make specialty lollipop and cake stands, which are an easy way to display cake pops and small cookie pops. Some are made to assist in the decoration process, and some are purely decorative. Wilton has a few decorative ones available.

Plates to Hold Upside-Down Pops

Upside-down pops are a breeze to display; just line them up on a plate with the sticks upright and you're ready to go. But not all plates are created equal. Pops look fabulous displayed on a rectangular or square plate, and for an extra special touch, you can cut decorative paper to line the plate. If the treats might stick to the decorative paper, you can top it with a layer of parchment paper cut the same size.

Platters

You don't have to arrange each and every treat on a stick so they all reach up to the sky; you can simply lay them down on large platters. Sometimes this is the best option when lots of kids will be grabbing their own treats, as it will minimize the risk of knocking over your display. You can still jazz up the plate with candy sprinkles, decorative paper, and most of the other suggestions in this chapter. Or you can use a combination of techniques, with a small upright display showing off your creativity sitting behind the easy-to-reach sweets on the platter.

Pop Gift Boxes

Cardboard boxes with see-through panels and special inserts to hold up your cake pops are available to purchase from specialty stores and make an easy way to display your treats for gift giving. Refer to Appendix A for a listing of speciality cake suppliers.

Toppings for Decorative Pails and Boxes

Cover up any messy-looking Styrofoam in containers with one of these fun embellishments. As usual, you will need to ensure that small children are monitored carefully around small items.

Candy

Bright-colored candy is one of the most eye-catching toppings you can use. Gumballs, chocolate-covered raisins, candy hearts, marshmallows—be guided by the treat on a stick and match up the candy color and shape accordingly.

Fruit or Vegetables

Any small bright fruit or vegetables—strawberries, cherries, grapes, peas still in the pod—will add a stimulating and tasteful touch to your display of sweet treats on a stick.

Paper Shred

A quick and easy topping, paper shred scrunched onto the top of your decorative display will look great, especially for cowboy and farm-themed treats.

Small Toys

Pile a stack of similar clean plastic animals or cars on top of your treat holder for an extra-quirky and unusual adornment. Many such toys can be bought reasonably at discount or toy stores and can double as gifts afterward.

Buttons, Beads, and Shells

Bags of shells, buttons, and beads can be picked up at craft or discount stores and make a charming display around your sweet treats.

Fabric or Dried Flowers

A layer of flowers can look very effective. If they have stems, you can insert them directly into the Styrofoam block; otherwise, just pile them on top in a decorative pattern.

The Finishing Touch

Add on that something extra to make your display really special. Do you have a plastic spider or skeleton sitting around from Halloween? Put it in the middle of your pail. Pop some artificial butterflies and bees in with your flower cookies. Be inspired by the treat you are displaying. Kids are particularly great at finding crazy ideas that end up working really well, so give them free rein on this task (with final approval from you to check on safety issues).

Name Cards and Other Tips

If you have a variety of treats to offer, it's a great idea to write or print out tags with the treat names and descriptions—for example, Moo Free Cake-Pops. You can even detail the ingredients, which is especially helpful when you have allergy suffers attending parties.

To help keep your treats fresh, you can wrap them in small plastic treat bags and secure them tightly with ribbon, twine, or pretty decorated tape. The bags are available from craft stores and come in various sizes.

Appendix A

Suppliers and Mail-Order Sources

Bake It Pretty

www.bakeitpretty.com

Sprinkles, baking cups, cookie cutters, candy coating, food color, pretty packaging, sugar decorations, cupcake toppers

Sugarcraft

www.sugarcraft.com

Lollipop sticks, sprinkles, baking cups, cookie cutters, fondant cutters, food color, lollipop stands, candy coating, luster spray, sugar decorations

Pastry Pedestal

www.thepastrypedestal.com

Pastry pedestals

Cake Art

www.cakeart.com

Lollipop sticks, sprinkles, baking cups, cookie cutters, fondant cutters, food color, candy coating, luster spray, sugar decorations

Kitchen Krafts

www.kitchenkrafts.com

Lollipop sticks, sprinkles, baking cups, cookie cutters, fondant cutters, food color, candy coating, luster spray, sugar decorations, cake pop gift boxes

Babycakes

http://thebabycakesshop.com/products/all

Cake pop maker, cake pop stand, lollipop sticks, and other accessories

Wilton

www.wilton.com

Wilton products

Michael's

www.michaels.com

Cookie cutters, Styrofoam blocks, fondant cutters, candy coating, lollipop sticks, food color, baking cups, sprinkles, sugar decorations, decorative papers, and pails for displaying

Hobby Lobby

www.hobbylobby.com

Cookie cutters, Styrofoam blocks, fondant cutters, candy coating, lollipop sticks, food color, baking cups, sprinkles, sugar decorations, decorative papers, and pails for displaying

A.C. Moore

www.acmoore.com

Cookie cutters, Styrofoam blocks, fondant cutters, candy coating, lollipop sticks, food color, baking cups, sprinkles, sugar decorations, decorative papers, and pails for displaying

Candy Warehouse

www.candywarehouse.com

Wide range of candy including gummy fish and Halloween candy

Ecrandal

www.ecrandal.com

Specialty and custom-made cookie cutters

Amazon

www.amazon.com

Etsy

www.etsy.com

When buying from Etsy you are buying from individuals; make sure to read the site terms of use and check feedback for each seller.

eBay

www.ebay.com

When buying from eBay you are buying from individuals; make sure to read the site terms of use and check feedback for each seller.

Canada

Scoop-N-Save

www.scoop-n-save.com

Australia

Little Betsy Baker

www.littlebetsybaker.com.au/store/pc/home.asp

Baking Pleasures

http://bakingpleasures.com.au

Cakes Around Town

www.cakesaroundtown.com.au

Appendix B

CONVERSION TABLE

1 teaspoon	5 milliliters
1 tablespoon	15 milliliters
1 fluid ounce	30 milliliters
¼ cup	60 milliliters
⅓ cup	80 milliliters
½ cup	120 milliliters
1 cup	240 milliliters
1 pint (2 cups)	480 milliliters
1 quart (4 cups)	960 milliliters
1 gallon (4 quarts)	3.84 liters
1 ounce (by weight)	28 grams
4 ounces	114 grams
8 ounces (½ pound)	228 grams
1 pound	454 grams
2.2 pounds	1 kilogram (1,000 grams)

DESCRIPTION	FAHRENHEIT	CELSIUS
Cool	200	90
Very Slow	250	120
Slow	300–325	150–160
Moderately Slow	325–350	160–180
Moderate	350–375	180–190
Moderately Hot	375–400	190–200
Hot	400–450	200–230
Very Hot	450–500	230–260

Index